archaeology

CITIES, EMPIRES, RELIGION, MIGRATIONS OF THE PAST

NATIONAL
GEOGRAPHIC
LEARNING

CENGAGE
Learning

Archaeology: Cities, Empires, Religion, Migrations of the Past

© 2014 National Geographic Learning, Cengage Learning

Photographic Credit: cover
© Vincent J. Musi/National Geographic Image Collection

For product information and technology assistance, contact us at
Cengage Learning Customer & Sales Support, 888-915-3276

For permission to use material from this text or product, submit all requests online at **www.cengage.com/permissions**. Further permissions questions can be emailed to **permissionrequest@cengage.com**.

ISBN: 978-12854-31420

National Geographic Learning
1880 Oak Avenue, Suite 300
Evanston, IL 60201
USA

Cengage Learning products are represented in Canada by Nelson Education, Ltd.

Visit National Geographic Learning online at **NGL.cengage.com**
Visit our corporate website at **www.cengage.com**.

Printed in the USA.
RR Donnelley, Jefferson City, MO

12 13 14 15 16 17 18 19 20 21 22

10 9 8 7 6 5 4 3 2 1

Table *of* Contents

v   About the Series

vi Preface

2 The Pyramid Builders
27 Discussion Questions
    Archaeological Interpretations
    Paradigm Creation

28 The Birth of Religion
53 Discussion Questions
    Archaeological Interpretations
    Paradigm Creation

54 Beyond the Blue Horizon
69 Discussion Questions
    Archaeological Interpretations
    Paradigm Creation

70 Lofty Ambitions of the Inca
95 Discussion Questions
    Archaeological Interpretations
    Paradigm Creation

96 Divining Angkor
121 Discussion Questions
    Archaeological Interpretations
    Paradigm Creation

About the Series

Cengage Learning and National Geographic Learning are proud to present the *National Geographic Learning Reader Series*. This ground-breaking series is brought to you through an exclusive partnership with the National Geographic Society, an organization that represents a tradition of amazing stories, exceptional research, first-hand accounts of exploration, rich content, and authentic materials.

The series brings learning to life by featuring compelling images, media, and text from National Geographic. Through this engaging content, students develop a clearer understanding of the world around them. Published in a variety of subject areas, the *National Geographic Learning Reader Series* connects key topics in each discipline to authentic examples and can be used in conjunction with most standard texts or online materials available for your courses.

How the reader works

Each article is focused on one topic relevant to the discipline. The introduction provides context to orient students and focus questions that suggest ideas to think about while reading the selection. Rich photography, compelling images, and pertinent maps are amply used to further enhance understanding of the selections. The chapter culminating section includes discussion questions to stimulate both in-class discussion and out-of-class work.

An eBook will accompany each reader and will provide access to the text online with a media library that may include images, videos, and other content specific to each individual discipline.

Few organizations present this world, its people, places, and precious resources in a more compelling way than National Geographic. Through this reader series we honor the mission and tradition of National Geographic Society: to inspire people to care about the planet.

Archaeology is the study of past peoples through the investigation of material remains. A daunting task, it requires the application of a wide range of techniques and interpretative methods in order to further our understanding of humanity's past. Archaeologists routinely blend data drawn from the application of physical sciences-geology, chemistry, and physics—with information generated via historical research—anthropological analogies, and social theory. These divergent threads are woven together by archaeologists to reconstruct past environmental conditions, historical events, and human decisions; all of which form our understanding of how human societies have changed over time. By its very nature as an exploratory discipline, archaeology is continuously uncovering new information through ongoing fieldwork, laboratory research, and analysis of existing collections. Each new piece of information holds the possibility of furthering our understanding of the past, often in very revolutionary ways. Archaeology is a constantly evolving field of study in which new lines of inquiry, methods of analysis, and interpretations of the past are proposed and enacted around the world.

This National Geographic reader brings together a diverse group of investigations into the past and highlights how recent research is revolutionizing our understanding of human history. Each unit touches on a provocative theme within archaeological research, many of which are highly relevant to modern societies as well. Each investigation uses both traditional and cutting-edge archaeological techniques and methods to generate a rich dataset from which detailed, sometimes controversial reconstructions of the past are created. Often these reconstructions are debated within the units provided, highlighting the diversity of archaeological points of view as well as the evolution of the field as a whole. By providing access to the archaeological datasets, reconstructions, and interpretations, each unit challenges the reader to critically evaluate the arguments provided and to potentially generate their own understanding of the past and how it might be applied to the modern world.

The reader is made up of five units. The first is based on one of the most basic aspects of human history; the emergence of organized religion and its affect on community organization and structure. Recent archaeological research in Turkey has demonstrated that rather than being a side-effect of other human inventions, such as agriculture, religion was instead a driving force for social change. The second unit investigates one of the most remarkable aspects of human existence; our ability to discover, colonize, and inhabit almost every corner of the world. By looking at the spread of humanity across the Pacific Ocean islands, this unit examines humans' insatiable desire to explore and move beyond familiar bounds. The third unit provides an intimate look at one of the most iconic archaeological sites—the Egyptian pyramids. Unlike most investigations into monumental constructions which focus on the elite class who designed the pyramids, this unit focuses on the daily lives, health, and motivation of the common people who constructed the pyramids. The fourth unit poses questions about the acquisition and centralization of political, military, and economic power by highlighting recent archaeological research into the history of the Incan empire. The unit explains how Inca power was based not just on military might, but also on the ability to effectively organize information, labor, and cosmology. The fifth and final unit provides a portrait of how great societies often collapse under their own weight. Ongoing archaeological fieldwork at Angkor Wat suggests numerous, disconnected factors caused the collapse of this early city, including weather patterns, religious beliefs, and political fractionation. Both individually and as a whole these units are designed to provide insights into both the history of the human experience as well as how archaeologists recreate these histories.

THE PYRAMID BUILDERS

Most archaeological research into monumental architecture focuses on the resultant constructions or on the elite members of society that sponsored their creation. This article shifts the focus towards the lives of the laborers, their cosmological beliefs, living conditions, and medical histories to better understand the social conditions surrounding pyramid construction in ancient Egypt. The everyday workers, both men and women, apparently were not slaves, captured warriors, or foreigners, but were instead workers who were relatively well treated and may have chosen to dedicate their lives to erecting the pyramids.

When reading this article, you should focus on:

- What was daily life like for the people who built the pyramids? What might have motivated people to work on constructing the pyramids?

- What led us to develop our original understanding of who built the pyramids and how they accomplished that feat? How is recent archaeological work challenging this original understanding?

- What were the organizational challenges associated with having a large labor force and how did the ancient Egyptians overcome them?

- How do archaeologists and physical anthropologists reconstruct the health and living conditions of the Egyptians who constructed the pyramids?

THE
PYRAMID
BUILDERS

By Virginia Morell

Photographs by Kenneth Garrett

I paid them in beer and bread, and I made them make an oath that they were satisfied." So said Kai (left), a priest and judge, of the builders and craftsmen who created his tomb—and, perhaps, worked on the pyramids. According to Harvard University archaeologist Mark Lehner and Zahi Hawass, director of archaeology at Giza and currently a National Geographic explorer-in-residence, 20,000 to 30,000 workers toiled on Giza's monuments at any one time, quarrying massive blocks of limestone and hauling them by hand up inclined ramps on wooden sleds.

MORE THAN 4,000 YEARS AGO AT GIZA,

THREE GENERATIONS OF EGYPTIANS

CONSTRUCTED A SERIES OF

MONUMENTS OF UNSURPASSED GRANDEUR.

EXCAVATIONS NOW REVEAL THE LIVES OF THE LABORERS AND OVERSEERS WHO RAISED THESE ANCIENT WONDERS.

On a sand-covered hill outside Cairo near the three great pyramids at Giza, Egyptologist Zahi Hawass picks a path among small tombs built of mud and stone. Some of the graves are shaped like beehives; others are rectangular structures carved into the rocky cliffs or constructed of limestone blocks and adorned with hieroglyphics; and still others are little more than small lumps of earth, their tops and sides studded with broken chunks of granite and limestone. Hawass has brought a team of excavators with him, and the men stop beside one of these humble tombs, designated by them as Grave 53. Several similar graves lie to either side, but Hawass has earmarked 53 as his team's morning labor.

"It's something I wondered about for years," Hawass tells me, taking a seat on a nearby rock, while members of his crew dig carefully into the top of the mastaba, as these tombs are called. "Many times when I looked at the pyramids, I would ask myself about the workers

The pyramids **always take a visitor's breath away,** in part because of their size, shape, and beauty but also because of the mind-numbing amount of work they obviously entailed.

who built them. Where were they buried? Who were the men and women behind this great enterprise? Because of these graves, we have some clues."

Contrary to earlier conjectures—and some modern guidebooks—the pyramids were not built by slaves or foreigners, says the silver-haired Hawass. "That idea of the slaves came from Herodotus," the Greek historian and explorer, Hawass continues. Herodotus visited Egypt around 450 b.c., about 2,000 years after the pyramids were constructed, and was told that 100,000 men had been forced to *(Continued on page 10)*

Adapted from "The Pyramid Builders" by Virginia Morell: National Geographic Magazine, November 2001.

COPPER AGE

Aided by lung power, Egyptians smelted copper (above), the only metal available to them, and from it forged tools to build the pyramids of Khufu, Khafre, and Menkaure between about 2550 and 2470 b.c. Workers today (left) have iron that readily cuts stone, and restorers at Giza can dress blocks with sharp iron chisels that shave off pieces of limestone. The softer

copper tools of antiquity, such as this gad (right), which was driven into fractures to break rock, were frequently reshaped, and chisels had to be continually resharpened. Quarriers and masons cut grooves in hard stone by pulling copper blades back and forth over a layer of abrasive sand. They used stone picks to carve out channels around pieces of rock and fitted wooden levers into sculpted sockets to pry blocks of limestone free.

Mediterranean Sea

Alexandria

NILE DELTA

EGYPT

PYRAMIDS
AT GIZA

★ Cairo

Saqqara ■ Memphis

Dahshur

Nile

EUROPE ASIA
EGYPT Area
enlarged
AFRICA

0 mi   40
0 km   40
NG MAPS

© 2001/National Geographic Maps/National Geographic Image Collection

*Excavations on Cairo's westernmost outskirts
have revealed what Lehner calls a "royal
production center," at lower right, that fed and
equipped workers at Giza. To the left lies a
cemetery dug into a cliff containing, Hawass
believes, the pyramid builders' tombs.*

(Continued from page 5) toil as slaves on the Great Pyramid of the pharaoh Khufu.

But Hawass's 1990 discovery of this cemetery, along with archaeologist Mark Lehner's nearby excavations of what appears to be the ancient laborers' city, confirms what Egyptologists had come to suspect: Herodotus was misinformed. Ordinary Egyptian citizens built the pyramids, some working as conscripts on a rotating basis, others as full-time employees. Hawass and Lehner estimate that the feat—quarrying, transporting, and fashioning the seven million cubic yards of stone for the three pyramids and adjoining structures—was accomplished with a workforce of only 20,000 to 30,000 men. Each pyramid complex (a grouping of pyramid, temples, and tombs) was started when a pharaoh assumed the throne and stopped when he died. Thus the Giza monuments, which were constructed during the 4th-dynasty reigns of Kings Khufu, Khafre, and Menkaure (about 2550 to 2470 b.c.), required some 80 years to build.

From my seat beside Grave 53 I can see the pointed summits of the two largest pyramids the workers built: the tombs of Khufu and his son Khafre. The pyramids always take a visitor's breath away, in part because of their size, shape, and beauty but also because of the mind-numbing amount of work they obviously entailed. They were built of blocks of limestone and granite ranging from less than one to more than 40 tons, all hewed, moved, and set in place by human hands. The ancient Egyptians relied on neither complex machines nor animals (nor extraterrestrials) for any of this labor. And after they completed the core of a pyramid (which is primarily what we see today), they covered it with stones precisely fitted together and polished until the pyramids gleamed like jewels in the sun.

"They were proud of their work, yes," says Hawass when I comment on the evident

It's because they were not just building the tomb of their king. They were building Egypt. It was a national project, and everyone was a participant.

care the pyramid builders took in their craft. "It's because they were not just building the tomb of their king. They were building Egypt. It was a national project, and everyone was a participant. People we're finding in these graves were part of that national project," he adds, nodding toward the one at his feet. "Many of them were cutting, moving, and polishing the stones."

By now Hawass's men have removed the mud bricks and rocks covering the grave, and some of them are carefully spading into the sand below. Others stand in a line above the pit with buckets woven from rubber inner tubes. Most wear long robes and turbans. It's a little after eight o'clock in the morning on an Egyptian spring day, but already the sun is high and hot, the sky a white-blue. I try to find a little shade behind a mastaba. For the crewmen, however, the heat, dust, and sweat are nothing new, and one by one they move forward to lower their buckets into the grave, where a workman named Said Saleh is digging. He fills each bucket with sandy soil. And one by one the workers hoist up their buckets, then walk down the slope to dump the sand on a pile, which two archaeologists run through a sieve. There's a steady rhythm to their digging, hoisting, and dumping—a smaller version, I imagine, of the crews who pushed, pulled, and set the stones of the pyramids.

Within minutes the team's efforts reveal the dark, pulverized bits of what had once been a wooden coffin.

"That's rare," says Hawass. "Usually these people were too poor to afford something like this. Maybe he worked in a carpenter's shop or knew someone who did."

Beneath the bits of wood Saleh uncovers the skull and collarbones, stained a yellowish brown color from the decaying coffin, then the rest of the skeleton. It lies bent in the fetal position, as was the custom, with the face pointing east toward the rising sun and the top of the skull aligned to the north, where the pharaoh's spirit ascended each night to join the "imperishable" circumpolar stars.

Saleh uses a brush to gently sweep away the earth from the bones; later a physical anthropologist will collect them for study. Bits of linen still cling to some of the bones, suggesting that this person had been wrapped in a cloth before being placed in the coffin.

"The poorer people often did this as a kind of symbolic mummification," Hawass says. "It was expensive to be mummified, so almost no one could afford it. But you could have the idea of being mummified with a cloth like this."

On one side of the skeleton Saleh unearths a curved knife made from yellow flint and hands this to Hawass.

"Even the poorest people were given something to help them in the afterlife," Hawass says. "Maybe this fellow used a knife like this for cutting his meat."

Many workers were also buried with jars of beer, Hawass adds, picking up one such rough red-clay pot lying on top of a nearby grave. "They made a beer from barley, and that was their daily drink. They didn't want to be without it even in the afterlife, so they often put in one of these jars."

Unlike some of the other mastabas Hawass has excavated, Grave 53 isn't equipped for after-death beer drinking. Instead, the sieving team has found a handful of tiny bone and faience beads. One of the men pours them into Hawass's hand.

"Ah!" says Hawass, giving a broad smile. "Well, our worker this morning is a woman. We'll know for sure after her bones are studied. But I think we have a woman here. You

It was as if **they had vanished.** But how do you lose 100,000 people, to use Herodotus's estimate—or even 20,000 or 30,000 people.

see, as I said, all Egyptians—men and women—helped to build the pyramids."

When archaeologists first began excavating at Giza some 200 years ago, they naturally turned their attention to the pharaohs' and queens' pyramids, associated temples and tombs, and the Great Sphinx. The ancient Egyptians built all these classic monuments during the 4th dynasty of the Old Kingdom, a veritable golden age of art and architecture.

Ironically, despite their huge and elaborate buildings, relatively little is known about the three key 4th-dynasty pharaohs. If Egyptians of this period recorded the activities of the royal households on papyrus rolls, as they would later, the rolls have not survived. Researchers have only the vaguest idea of what Pharaoh Khufu, who built the Great Pyramid, looked like; one small ivory statue with his name inscribed has survived, and this may have been carved a few centuries after his death. Yet scientists know even less about the common people who toiled on the tombs and temples for the ruling elite.

"It was as if they had vanished," says Mark Lehner, who has spent the past decade searching for the pyramid builders' homes and workshops. "But how do you lose 100,000 people, to use Herodotus's estimate—or even 20,000 or 30,000 people?"

There were a few clues about this workforce, and Lehner leads me to one: the limestone quarries immediately below Menkaure's pyramid. "Here's one of the grooves they made to remove a block of stone," he says, bending down next to a channel five inches wide and three inches deep cut into the rock. "They worked with stone picks and copper chisels to free each block, and they carved out sockets for wooden levers so they could pop the whole block—a 20-ton rock—free." *(Continued on page 15)*

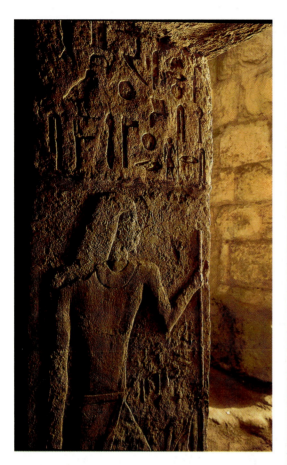

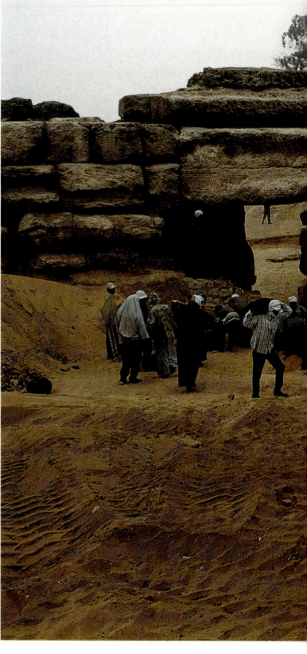

WALL OF THE CROW

Weser-Petah, described as the one whom the King knows, honored one by the Great God, and overseer of the officials, looks out on eternity from the doorway of his tomb in the upper section of the builders' cemetery. Raising the pyramids was as much a feat of organization as engineering. Administrators such as Weser-Petah had to coordinate the arrival of rotating teams of laborers and shipments of supplies from all over Egypt. A gateway in the Wall of the Crow (right) could have been used to manage the flow of goods and people from the sacred pyramid complex on the north to the royal production center on the south. Lehner and Hawass believe that the wall lay just south of a harbor linked to the Nile by canals and filled by the river's floods. Where excavators walk, carrying dirt from the wall's base, ancient stevedores may have bustled back and forth with loads of copper, fish, grain, wood, and cattle.

WATERS OF PLENTY

A fishseller's table in Cairo echoes the bounty of the ancient Nile, which fed the pyramid workers. Archaeologists have recovered the remains of a wide variety of freshwater fish from the royal production center. "They were out there catching everything they could," says Richard Redding, a bone specialist on Lehner's team. One building had benches where workers may have gutted larger fish. Floors were littered with tiny bones of small fish like those the men in a relief (left) pull from the shallows. These were probably dried, salted, and eaten whole. Seal impressions in clay (right) carry parts of the names of Khafre and Menkaure, the pharaohs who built the second and third pyramids at Giza.

(Continued from page 11) Each block was delineated with red paint before the workers began to remove it. "Some years ago you could still see traces of that red paint," says Lehner, "and a cartouche," the hieroglyphics that encircle someone's name. "It was probably the mark of the team of workers who had to quarry the block."

Similar team-name inscriptions have been found inside the pyramids. On two blocks in the highest chamber of Khufu's Great Pyramid, for example, a gang of workers painted hieroglyphics that read "Friends of Khufu." And in Menkaure's mortuary temple another group displayed its insignia: "Drunkards of Menkaure."

Those team names alone, I note, suggest something other than a slave mentality.

Lehner nods. A slightly built man in his 50s, he carries the tools of his archaeological trade—pens, trowel, tape measure, paintbrush—jutting from the pockets of his shirt and jeans.

"The workers were organized into competing teams," he explains, "which may have helped them psychologically. You know, 'Let's see whose team can do this job faster.'"

After all, he adds, much of the work the teams had to do was not fun. "Imagine working under the hot Egyptian sun with a stone pick or copper chisel to cut these blocks of stone and then pushing and pulling them to make a pyramid. How do we come to grips with making people work so hard? What motivated them? The most we can say, because we have so few papyrus texts from this period, is that they were deeply religious and believed that by building the tomb for their king, they were assuring his rebirth as well as their own and that of Egypt overall."

To build such monumental structures, the Egyptians needed a highly organized workforce. From tomb inscriptions and from laborers' instructions on walls inside Khufu's pyramid and Menkaure's mortuary temple, researchers can now draw something close to a modern personnel chart for the ancient workers. "Every project like a pyramid had a crew of workers," explains Ann Roth, an Egyptologist who has studied the groups of workers in detail. "And each group was responsible for one part of the pyramid complex. There was one group for building the interior granite roofs and separate groups for raising the chamber walls."

Each crew of workers was divided into four or five smaller units, which Egyptologists call *phyles* (after the Greek for "tribe"). Each phyle carried a name, such as "Great One" or "Green One." The phyles too were broken into forces of 10 to 20 men, and these had names like "Endurance" and "Perfection."

"They had to be very organized," says Lehner, "to build these things as quickly as they did." He notes that some researchers have calculated that in order to construct a pyramid in 20 years' time, the workers had to set a stone in place every two minutes. "It's a phenomenal pace."

To keep that kind of workforce functioning at top speed, a highly developed support force was also needed, notes Lehner. "You have to have a place to feed and house all these workers and the other workers—the bakers, brewers, and butchers—who support them."

In other words, you need a city. And Lehner thinks he has found it—or at least the production or industrial part of the city.

On a wide, sandy plain a few hundred yards below Hawass's cemetery, Lehner and his crew have excavated carefully thought-out—and paved—streets and well-designed buildings divided into small chambers and linked by corridors. Along the north side of this site a massive wall of hewn stone, the Heit el-Ghorab (Wall of the Crow), extends for some 600 feet. The wall rises nearly 33 feet, is 33 feet thick at its base, and has a center gate capped with three massive limestone lintels.

"We still aren't sure who passed through that gate or why it was there," says Lehner. We stand just at its portal, close to the area where members of his team are now excavating what he calls South Street. *(Continued on page 20)*

BEEF, BREAD, AND BEER

An ancient Egyptian seizes a calf so another man can milk its mother in a scene from the Old Kingdom (above). To provide meat for workers, officials collected large calves from farmers and received donations from wealthy estates in the lush cattle-raising region of the delta. Herders, such as these boys in Dahshur (left), drove cattle along the Nile toward Giza,

gathering more animals as they went. At the royal production center cattle were slaughtered in an industrial-scale food-processing operation that left remains scattered across the site (right, top to bottom): charcoal for cooking; emmer wheat for bread and barley for beer; a flint butcher knife; and teeth and bones from cattle, sheep, goats, and fish.

Standing before a false door built for the dead, Momadouh Taha, an archaeologist on Hawass's team, examines inscriptions in Nefer-Theith's tomb, one of the most elaborate in the builders' cemetery. Hieroglyphics identify Nefer-Theith as overseer of a palace, which was probably located nearby. Hawass thinks that he may have had another role: supervisor of bakeries. Tomb reliefs show workers grinding grain and baking bread.

Family and friends bear the shrouded body of an official's wife during a funeral in the builders' cemetery. Behind them walk a professional mourner and two white-sashed priests, one holding a prayer scroll, the other a pot of water for libations. As the grieving husband is comforted by his son, servants at the foot of a stairway sink to the ground and pull their hair. Beyond, life continues: Animals are brought to slaughter, and donkey trains carry supplies into the royal production center, which is overhung with smoke from scores of foundry and cooking fires.

(Continued from page 15) "It's our third such street here, and it runs parallel to the other two. It was a gridded city and quite unusual for its time." Prior to its discovery some Egyptologists thought that settlements in Old Kingdom days would have been nothing more than expanded villages, with streets and work areas placed in a higgledy-piggledy fashion. "We helped put the kibosh on that idea," says Lehner.

He knows that several buildings were used as bakeries, others as breweries. But Lehner is still unsure about the industrial area's overall purpose. "Was it here solely to feed the workers?" he asks, leaning down to sweep away the sand from a tiny fish spine. "Or did they use buildings like this one, where we've found so many fish bones, to prepare offerings for the temples?"

Again, there are no papyrus texts or wall inscriptions—not even any ancient graffiti—to give an answer. The only textual clues to the site come from tiny scraps of sealing clay that once secured the mouths of jars of wine and oil or sacks of grain.

In a lab near Lehner's excavation Egyptologist John Nolan hands me a magnifying lens to

take a closer look at one such scrap. It's flat and dark brown, and along the surface it bears the tiny imprints of hieroglyphics—as well as the fine lines of someone's fingerprints. On this one the symbol of a falcon with folded wings clearly stands out. "That's a sign that this is the name of a king, in this case Menkaure," says Nolan. "It implies that the person who made this was a high official."

The imprints were made by rolling a carved seal over a piece of wet clay to create a sealing. After someone had filled a jar, say, with wine, the mouth of the jar was covered with a piece of cloth and tied with a cord, and the moist clay sealing was put in place. The sealings, Nolan adds, were like little tags attached to commodities. "Sealed goods were the closest thing to money these people had. The sealings established a chain of responsibility: There was the person who put the sealing on and the person with the authority to break it."

Nolan has thousands of these sealing scraps left to read. Stored in plastic bags, they line his desk like micromystery tales. "There's always the chance that I'll (Continued on page 24)

FINAL MONUMENTS

Four statues portray aspects of the life of Inty-Shedu, a carpenter who Hawass believes oversaw the manufacture of wooden tools and boats at Giza. The people buried in the builders' cemetery modeled their tombs on those of the pharaohs. Inty-Shedu's group of statues, discovered in the upper part of the cemetery reserved for officials and artisans, is similar to ones found in pyramid temples. In the lower part of the cemetery, Hawass (right, at far right) sits on a mud-and-stone mastaba, or tomb, belonging to one of many workers buried beside their overseers. Some tombs are dome-shaped and, like the pyramids, evoke the mythical mound of creation. Causeways, at top, link the upper and lower cemetery and resemble those connecting the Nile Valley to the pyramids. An Old Kingdom text expresses the builders' hope in the afterlife: "Make good your dwelling in the graveyard; make worthy your station in the west."

(Continued from page 21) find one with a title we recognize—someone besides the king. Maybe there'll be one that ties our site directly to the workers' cemetery."

Finding such a link would clear up a question about how closely Hawass's cemetery and Lehner's city are connected in time. Lehner's site has been dated to the mid to late 4th dynasty, and Hawass thinks his cemetery runs from the mid-4th dynasty into the 5th. Yet even if the two sites are not intimately connected, the workers' tombs have given archaeologists a better understanding of the organization that lay behind the building of the pyramids.

Although most of the graves are those of poor workers, several mark the resting places of more important—and wealthy—officials. Some of these are built like miniature versions of the temples of the kings and queens. They are rectangular and made of limestone blocks, and they have all the key features a tomb should have: carved false doors for the person's spirit to use to exit the tomb each night, stone offering basins, and hieroglyphic inscriptions giving the owner's name and title as well as the names of his wife and children. Two even have ramps leading up to their doorways, like the long causeways outside the three pyramids.

The owners of these two tombs "wanted them to look as much like those of their pharaohs as possible," says Hawass, walking up one of the ramps. "This one is the tomb of Weser-Petah, overseer of the officials." The ramp leads to a small doorway. I bend down and step inside the carved-rock tomb. It is a simple structure, like a narrow but shortened railroad car. Above the false door and on either side of it are bas-reliefs showing Weser-Petah in the classic Egyptian profile and beside and below them hieroglyphics spelling his name and title. Although not as elaborate as the tomb inscriptions of the ruling elite, these carvings still reveal the care and concern the Egyptians had for assuring a good afterlife.

A few steps to the west takes us to the ramp and tomb of Ni-ankh-Petah, overseer of the king's bakeries and cakes, and uphill from his tomb stands that of Nefer-Theith, overseer of the palace and purifier of the king. Other tombs bear such titles as overseer of the rowers, overseer of the side of the pyramid, inspector of the royal gardens, and master of the harbor. So far, Hawass's team has discovered 26 of these titles.

"The titles are those of mid- to high-level managers," notes Hawass, "and further demonstrate the tight organization of the ancient Egyptian workforce."

"That's what really blossomed in the 4th dynasty," says Egyptologist James Allen. "It wasn't the discovery of how to work large blocks of stone; it was the discovery of how to organize a large labor force."

Many elite women were buried in the tombs of their husbands, and often they too had their names and titles inscribed on the lintels of the false doorways, as did the wife of Petty, inspector of the craftsmen. Her name was Nesy-Sokar, and she was a priestess of Hathor, goddess of love and dance. Two women had their own tombs; one, like Nesy-Sokar, was a priestess of Hathor and the other a priestess of Neith, goddess of war.

Like the pharaohs, these titled officials—men and women—often had various goods placed in their tombs to help them in the afterlife. There might be beer jars as well as miniature offering plates and drinking cups, but these were made of clay and about the size of a child's tea party set. "There was nothing of real value in these tombs," says Hawass, "which is why they were not looted." That did not prevent the tomb owners from worrying about thieves. Below the exquisitely etched portraits of Petty and Nesy-Sokar a row of protective curses was carved, threatening harm to anyone who disturbed their resting place.

"As for any person, male or female, who shall do evil against this tomb and who shall enter therein, the crocodile shall be against him upon water, the hippopotamus shall be

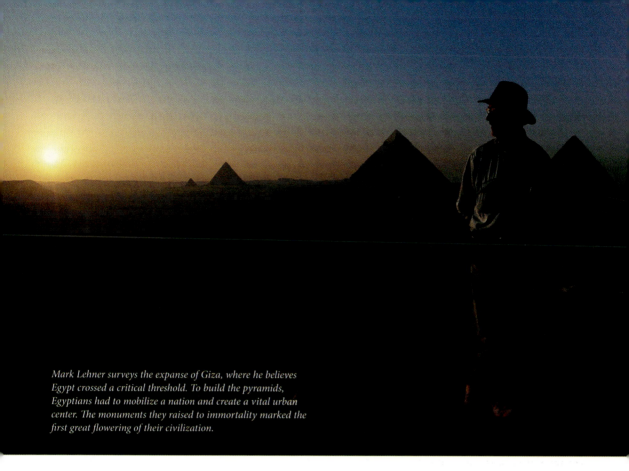

Mark Lehner surveys the expanse of Giza, where he believes Egypt crossed a critical threshold. To build the pyramids, Egyptians had to mobilize a nation and create a vital urban center. The monuments they raised to immortality marked the first great flowering of their civilization.

against him in the water, and the scorpion shall be against him on land."

Some of the tombs contained small statues of their owners. Most of these, such as the statue of Nefer-ef-Nesu, chief of the sculptors, and his wife Nefer-Menkhes, were carved from limestone, then painted. The statue shows the couple seated side by side on a bench of "pink granite"—the limestone has been painted in trompe l'oeil fashion to resemble that royal rock. She wears a fancy net dress, a beaded necklace, and bracelets, while he is dressed in a simple white kilt. They both face forward, with slight beatific smiles, and she has her right arm around her husband's shoulder. "It is their ideal, how they want to be in the afterlife," says Tarek El-Awady, an archaeologist and assistant to Hawass. "So they want to look their best and wear the best clothes and jewelry."

For most of these fancy tomb owners daily life in Egypt was probably not too difficult. Surrounded by desert and blessed with fertile land and crops, Old Kingdom Egypt was a rare place: a state marked by sufficient peace and stability so that there was ample leisure and wealth to cultivate a culture devoted to the afterlife. But even the Egyptians faced disease, old age, and death, and for the laborers life was surely hard.

"We can see that in their skeletons," says Azza Mohamed Sarry El-Din, a physical anthropologist who is studying the skeletal remains from the cemetery. "I've looked at 175 skeletons so far, about half men, half women, and nearly all of them suffered from arthritis. Their lumbar vertebrae are badly compressed, as you would expect for a manual workforce. I expected to see that—but I was surprised to see this kind of arthritis in the women too." She lays out the neck and lumbar vertebrae of one woman who died in her early 30s and points to the roughened, eroded edges of the bones. "She must have been carrying heavy loads on her head from the time she was a young girl to get this kind of damage," says Sarry El-Din.

Although there are no records or carvings showing women pushing stones or pulling statues on sleds (as there are of men doing this kind of labor), the condition of the women's bones suggests to her that they were. "There is more damage to their bones than you would expect from simply doing household chores"— or from supporting weight on their heads.

Some of the skeletons also suggest that the workers, despite the hard nature of their occupations, were well treated, although they may not have had the best diet—Sarry El-Din's initial analysis suggests that some individuals were anemic and that most of the laborers ate very little meat. (Curiously, Lehner's team has excavated great quantities of bones from butchered cattle, sheep, and goats—more than enough, he says, to feed several thousand workers some meat each day. Were the slaughtered animals intended only as offerings for the temple cults? The discrepancy between bones, diet, and quantities of meat remains a mystery.) But the workers did have access to good medical care. One worker suffered a badly injured arm, which a doctor amputated below the elbow; the operation healed as well as a similar amputation performed on the leg of an official. "Both men recovered and lived for many years after their accidents," says Sarry El-Din. "Someone was taking care of these laborers. Workers who are pushing stones around like this are going to be hurt, and it's heartening to see that their overseers knew this and had a clinic for them."

Despite the availability of medical care the workers' lives were short. On average a man lived 40 to 45 years, a woman 30 to 35. "The women's lives were shorter, probably because of problems in childbirth," says Sarry El-Din. "But very few people were living what we think of as a long life."

Yet they wanted to. They loved life, Egyptologists say, and their elaborate funeral industry was aimed at one thing: assuring that life never ended.

"You could look at this as a fairly miserable existence," Lehner says, standing on a bluff above his site. "There would have been hundreds of fires burning to bake the bread, to make the pottery and copper chisels, and to keep those chisels sharpened. The air was probably thick with smoke, and there were people moving in long lines to pull the blocks to the pyramid site and people grinding grains, butchering cattle, probably unloading goods in a harbor we think was close to the pyramids. It was all hard, hot, sweaty labor."

And what did it get you? "It gave you a job, a way of making a living, and it gave you a national purpose. And, for them at least, it gave them life beyond this world."

Discussion Questions:

- How has the recent archaeological research highlighted in the article changed our understanding of who built the Egyptian pyramids?

- According to the article, what might have motivated the labor crews to construct the pyramids?

- What are the greatest challenges associated with constructing large-scale architecture such as the pyramids?

- What does this article suggest in terms of social hierarchy in ancient Egypt? What sort of divisions exist, how are they visible in the archaeological record, and how might this compare to current social hierarchy in the United States?

Archaeological Interpretations:

- What kind of information did archaeologists and physical anthropologists rely on in order to reconstruct the living conditions, health, and medical histories of the Egyptians who built the pyramids?

- How did the results of these findings influence our understanding of the social conditions surrounding the creation of the pyramids and the socio-political status of the individuals involved in that creation?

- How do you think these new interpretations of pyramid construction might potentially affect our larger understanding of ancient Egypt? In particular, how does this article challenge the traditional understanding of Egypt by focusing on commoners rather than elites?

Paradigm Creation:
Elite Dominance and the Power of the Commoners

- What were some of the physical challenges associated with creating monumental architecture highlighted in *The Pyramid Builders?* What were the social challenges associated with organizing such a large group of laborers? How were these challenges met?

- How does shifting the focus of archaeological research away from the elites of ancient Egypt towards the rest of the population change our understanding of this past culture? How does it challenge our interpretation of not only how the pyramids were built, but also what they meant to ancient Egyptians?

THE BIRTH OF RELIGION

Archaeologists have long thought that agriculture was an important precursor to organized religion, sedentism, and social complexity. This article offers recent research at Göbekli Tepe, a 11,600-year-old site in Turkey, which suggests that organized religion predates agriculture. Archaeologists suggest that Göbekli Tepe was a place where dispersed hunter-gatherer groups gathered for rituals and feasting, which was a basis for the cosmological and ideological shifts that we recognize as organized religion. Research is ongoing at Göbekli Tepe, and there is much left to discover, including how it changed through time and its eventual disuse.

When reading this article, you should focus on:

- What is the traditional understanding of the timing of the rise of agriculture, sedentism, and religion? How does Göbekli Tepe fit into this traditional understanding?
- What is the relationship between organized religion and agriculture?
- What is meant by organized religion?
- How do seemingly unrelated social practices, such as gathering crops and sedentism, relate to one another?

Pillars at the temple of Göbekli Tepe in southern Turkey—11,600 years old and up to 18 feet tall—may represent priestly dancers at a gathering. Note the hands above the loincloth-draped belt on the figure in the foreground.

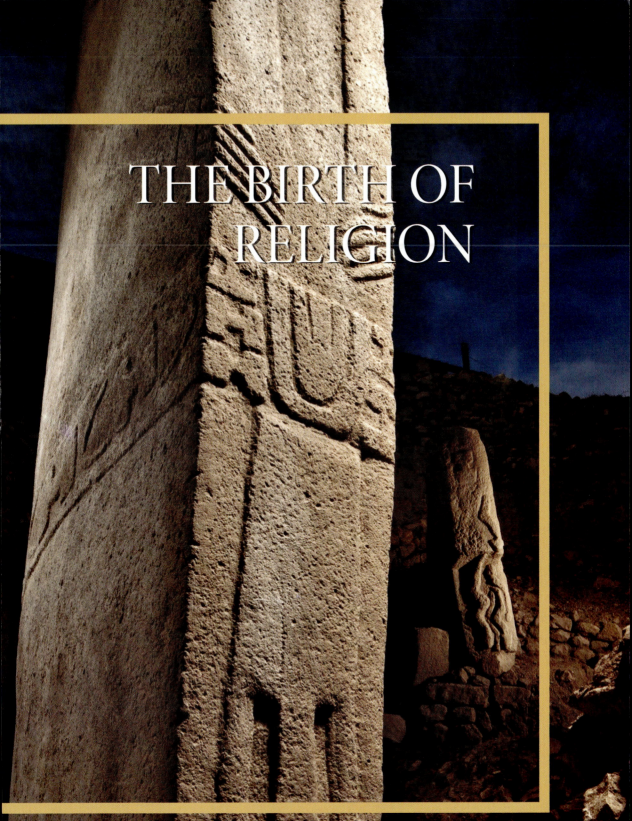

THE BIRTH OF RELIGION

A snarling predator erupts from a five-ton piece of limestone, which artisans moved to Göbekli Tepe from a nearby quarry without the aid of draft animals or wheels.

WE USED TO THINK AGRICULTURE GAVE RISE TO CITIES AND LATER TO WRITING, ART, AND RELIGION. NOW

THE WORLD'S OLDEST TEMPLE

SUGGESTS THE URGE TO WORSHIP SPARKED CIVILIZATION.

Every now and then the dawn of civilization is reenacted on a remote hilltop in southern Turkey.

The reenactors are busloads of tourists—usually Turkish, sometimes European. The buses (white, air-conditioned, equipped with televisions) blunder over the winding, indifferently paved road to the ridge and dock like dreadnoughts before a stone portal. Visitors flood out, fumbling with water bottles and MP3 players. Guides call out instructions and explanations. Paying no attention, the visitors straggle up the hill. When they reach the top, their mouths flop open with amazement, making a line of perfect cartoon O's.

Before them are dozens of massive stone pillars arranged into a set of rings, one mashed up against the next. Known as Göbekli Tepe (pronounced Guh-behk-LEE teh-peh), the site is vaguely reminiscent of Stonehenge, except that Göbekli Tepe was built much earlier and is made not from roughly hewn blocks but from cleanly carved limestone pillars splashed with bas-reliefs of animals—a

The new research suggests that the "revolution" was actually carried out by many hands across a huge area and over thousands of years.

cavalcade of gazelles, snakes, foxes, scorpions, and ferocious wild boars. The assemblage was built some 11,600 years ago, seven millennia before the Great Pyramid of Giza. It contains the oldest known temple. Indeed, Göbekli Tepe is the oldest known example of monumental architecture—the first structure human beings put together that was bigger and more complicated than a hut. When these pillars were erected, so far as we know, nothing of comparable scale existed in the world.

At the time of Göbekli Tepe's construction much of the human race lived in small nomadic bands that survived by foraging for plants and hunting wild animals. Construction of the site would have required more people coming together in one place than had likely occurred before. Amazingly, the temple's builders were able to cut, shape, and transport 16-ton stones hundreds of feet despite having no wheels or beasts of *(Continued on page 34)*

(Continued on page 34)

Adapted from "The Birth of Religion" by Charles C. Mann: National Geographic Magazine, June 2011.

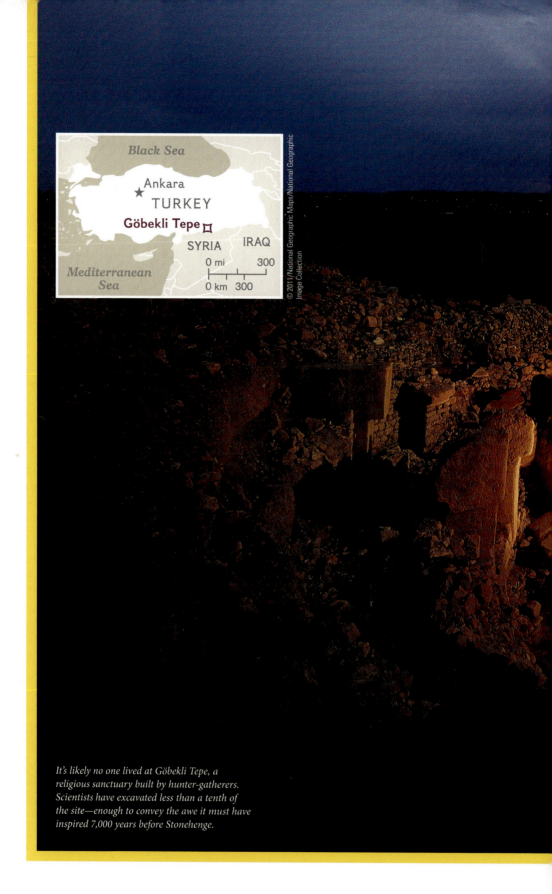

Black Sea

Ankara
★
TURKEY

Göbekli Tepe ⌂

SYRIA   IRAQ

0 mi   300

0 km   300

Mediterranean
Sea

It's likely no one lived at Göbekli Tepe, a religious sanctuary built by hunter-gatherers. Scientists have excavated less than a tenth of the site—enough to convey the awe it must have inspired 7,000 years before Stonehenge.

(Continued from page 31) burden. The pilgrims who came to Göbekli Tepe lived in a world without writing, metal, or pottery; to those approaching the temple from below, its pillars must have loomed overhead like rigid giants, the animals on the stones shivering in the firelight—emissaries from a spiritual world that the human mind may have only begun to envision.

Archaeologists are still excavating Göbekli Tepe and debating its meaning. What they do know is that the site is the most significant in a volley of unexpected findings that have overturned earlier ideas about our species' deep past. Just 20 years ago most researchers believed they knew the time, place, and rough sequence of the Neolithic Revolution—the critical transition that resulted in the birth of agriculture, taking Homo sapiens from scattered groups of hunter-gatherers to farming villages and from there to technologically sophisticated societies with great temples and towers and kings and priests who directed the labor of their subjects and recorded their feats in written form. But in recent years multiple new discoveries, Göbekli Tepe preeminent among them, have begun forcing archaeologists to reconsider.

At first the Neolithic Revolution was viewed as a single event—a sudden flash of genius—that occurred in a single location, Mesopotamia, between the Tigris and Euphrates Rivers in what is now southern Iraq, then spread to India, Europe, and beyond. Most archaeologists believed this sudden blossoming of civilization was driven largely by environmental changes: a gradual warming as the Ice Age ended that allowed some people to begin cultivating plants and herding animals in abundance. The new research suggests that the "revolution" was actually carried out by many hands across a huge area and over thousands of years. And it may have been driven not by the environment but by something else entirely.

After a moment of stunned quiet, tourists at the site busily snap pictures with cameras and cell phones. Eleven millennia ago nobody had digital imaging equipment, of course. Yet things have changed less than one might think. Most of the world's great religious centers, past and present, have been destinations for pilgrimages—think of the Vatican, Mecca, Jerusalem, Bodh Gaya (where Buddha was enlightened), or Cahokia (the enormous Native American complex near St. Louis). They are monuments for spiritual travelers, who often came great distances, to gawk at and be stirred by. Göbekli Tepe may be the first of all of them, the beginning of a pattern. What it suggests, at least to the archaeologists working there, is that the human sense of the sacred—and the human love of a good spectacle—may have given rise to civilization itself.

Klaus Schmidt knew almost instantly that he was going to be spending a lot of time at Göbekli Tepe. Now a researcher at the German Archaeological Institute (DAI), Schmidt had spent the autumn of 1994 trundling across southeastern Turkey. He had been working at a site there for a few years and was looking for another place to excavate. The biggest city in the area is Şanlıurfa (pronounced shan-lyoor-fa). By the standards of a brash newcomer like London, Şanlıurfa is incredibly old—the place where the Prophet Abraham supposedly was born. Schmidt was in the city to find a place that would help him understand the Neolithic, a place that would make Şanlıurfa look young. North of Şanlıurfa the ground ripples into the first foothills of the mountains that run across southern Turkey, source of the famous Tigris and Euphrates Rivers. Nine miles outside of town is a long ridge with a rounded crest that locals call Potbelly Hill—Göbekli Tepe.

In the 1960s archaeologists from the University of Chicago had surveyed the region and concluded that Göbekli Tepe was of little interest. Disturbance was evident at the top of the hill, but they attributed it to the activities of a Byzantine-era military outpost. Here and there were broken pieces of limestone they thought were gravestones. Schmidt had come across the Chicago researchers' brief description of the hilltop and decided to check it out. On the ground he saw flint chips—huge numbers of them. "Within minutes of getting there," Schmidt says, he realized that he was looking at a place where scores or even hundreds of people had worked in millennia past. The limestone slabs were not Byzantine graves but something much older. In collaboration with the DAI and the Şanlıurfa Museum, he set to work the next year.

Inches below the surface the team struck an elaborately fashioned stone. Then another, and another—a ring of standing pillars. As the months and years went by, Schmidt's team, a shifting crew of German and Turkish graduate students and 50 or more local villagers, found a second circle of stones, then a third, and then more. Geomagnetic surveys in 2003 revealed at least 20 rings piled together, higgledy-piggledy, under the earth.

The pillars were big—the tallest are 18 feet in height and weigh 16 tons. Swarming over their surfaces was a menagerie of animal bas-reliefs, each in a different style, some roughly rendered, a few as refined and symbolic as Byzantine art. Other parts of the hill were *(Continued on page 42)*

PATHS TO CIVILIZATION

Göbekli Tepe and other sites in the Middle East are changing ideas about how itinerant bands of hunter-gatherers settled into village life as farmers—a turning point in history called the Neolithic Revolution. Two theories about this transition, which unfolded over thousands of years, are outlined below.

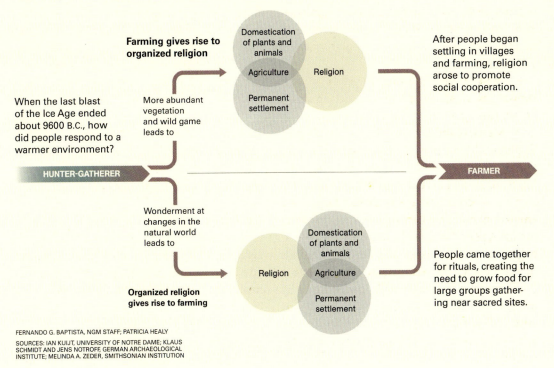

FERNANDO G. BAPTISTA, NGM STAFF; PATRICIA HEALY

SOURCES: IAN KUIJT, UNIVERSITY OF NOTRE DAME; KLAUS SCHMIDT AND JENS NOTROFF, GERMAN ARCHAEOLOGICAL INSTITUTE; MELINDA A. ZEDER, SMITHSONIAN INSTITUTION

WHERE FARMING BEGAN

The Fertile Crescent was the heartland of the Neolithic Revolution. Göbekli Tepe sat on the northern edge of this region that curves along the boundary between mountain and desert, rich in the wild grasses and game that became the first domesticated grains and livestock. By 6000 B.C. the transformation from hunter-gatherers to farmers was largely complete in this area. As selected sites on the map show, this shift—whether driven by religious rituals, environmental changes, or population pressures—happened in different places and at different times.

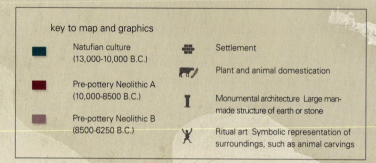

key to map and graphics

■ Natufian culture (13,000-10,000 B.C.)

■ Pre-pottery Neolithic A (10,000-8500 B.C.)

■ Pre-pottery Neolithic B (8500-6250 B.C.)

▦ Settlement

🐂 Plant and animal domestication

𝕀 Monumental architecture Large man-made structure of earth or stone

⥕ Ritual art Symbolic representation of surroundings, such as animal carvings

Mediterranean

Wild wheat

Domesticated wheat

Plumper kernels distinguish domesticated grains from their wild ancestors. Wild kernels drop off when ripe, but domesticated strains hold their kernels, allowing a more predictable harvest.

EGYPT

0 mi — 100
0 km — 100

Present-day boundaries, rivers, and shorelines shown

Nile

Warm, wet climate   Cold, dry climate

NATUFIAN CULTURE

|13,000 B.C. |12,000 |11,000

The rise of village life
Early hunter-gatherer settlements—some with several hundred people—were largely abandoned when the warming climate chilled again for 1,200 years. About 9600 B.C. temperatures rose and villages rebounded, with people still foraging for most of their food and sharing it. As farming took hold and village populations increased, individual families fed themselves.

In Natufian settlements (named for a site where they were first excavated) hunter-gatherers built stacked-stone huts, probably roofed with animal hides.

Estimated average community size, based on studies in the southwest Fertile Crescent.

☐
■ 18 people

Communal area

FERNANDO G. BAPTISTA, NGM STAFF; PATRICIA HEALY; DEBBIE GIBBONS, NG STAFF (MAP)

SOURCES: IAN KUIJT, UNIVERSITY OF NOTRE DAME; KLAUS SCHMIDT, JENS NOTROFF, AND OLIVER DIETRICH, GERMAN ARCHAEOLOGICAL INSTITUTE; GEORGE WILLCOX, NATIONAL CENTER FOR SCIENTIFIC RESEARCH, FRANCE; MELINDA A. ZEDER, SMITHSONIAN INSTITUTION

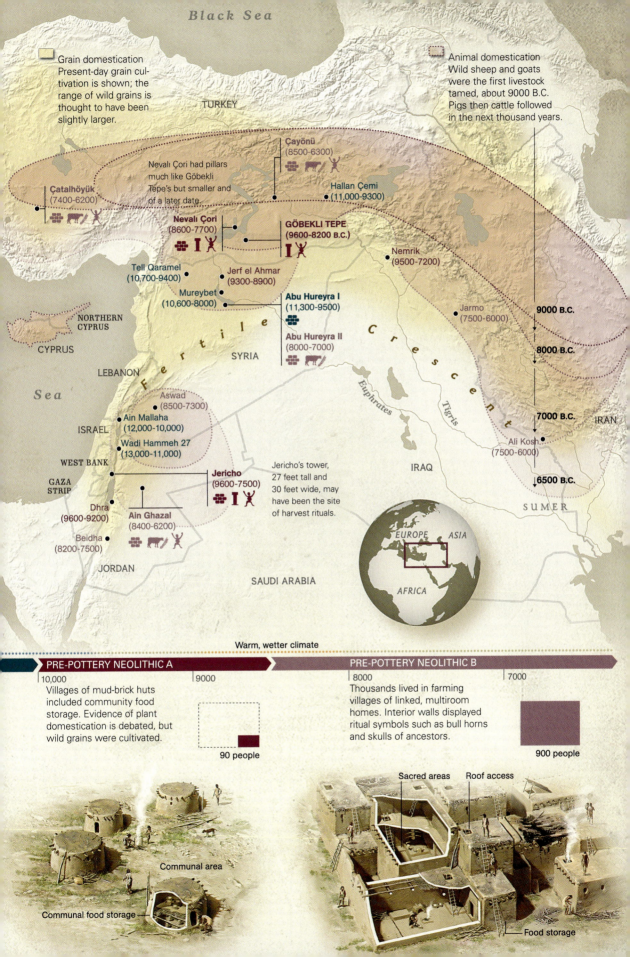

Black Sea

Grain domestication
Present-day grain cultivation is shown; the range of wild grains is thought to have been slightly larger.

Animal domestication
Wild sheep and goats were the first livestock tamed, about 9000 B.C. Pigs then cattle followed in the next thousand years.

TURKEY

Çayönü
(8500-6300)

Çatalhöyük
(7400-6200)

Nevalı Çori had pillars much like Göbekli Tepe's but smaller and of a later date.

Hallan Çemi
(11,000-9300)

Nevalı Çori
(8600-7700)

GÖBEKLI TEPE
(9600-8200 B.C.)

Nemrik
(9500-7200)

Tell Qaramel
(10,700-9400)

Jerf el Ahmar
(9300-8900)

Mureybet
(10,600-8000)

Abu Hureyra I
(11,300-9500)

Jarmo
(7500-6000)

9000 B.C.

NORTHERN CYPRUS

Fertile

Abu Hureyra II
(8000-7000)

SYRIA

8000 B.C.

CYPRUS

Crescent

Euphrates

Tigris

LEBANON

Sea

Aswad
(8500-7300)

7000 B.C.

IRAN

Ain Mallaha
(12,000-10,000)

ISRAEL

Ali Kosh
(7500-6000)

Wadi Hammeh 27
(13,000-11,000)

WEST BANK

Jericho
(9600-7500)

IRAQ

6500 B.C.

GAZA STRIP

Jericho's tower, 27 feet tall and 30 feet wide, may have been the site of harvest rituals.

SUMER

Dhra
(9600-9200)

Ain Ghazal
(8400-6200)

EUROPE   ASIA

Beidha
(8200-7500)

AFRICA

JORDAN

SAUDI ARABIA

Warm, wetter climate

PRE-POTTERY NEOLITHIC A

10,000   9000

Villages of mud-brick huts included community food storage. Evidence of plant domestication is debated, but wild grains were cultivated.

90 people

PRE-POTTERY NEOLITHIC B

8000   7000

Thousands lived in farming villages of linked, multiroom homes. Interior walls displayed ritual symbols such as bull horns and skulls of ancestors.

900 people

Communal area

Communal food storage

Sacred areas   Roof access

Food storage

BUILDING GÖBEKLI TEPE

People must have gathered from far-flung settlements to erect the first known temples. Using flint tools, they carved pillars and shaped blocks for walls mortared with clay. When a new temple was completed, the old one was buried. How the temples were used is unknown.

Head

Arm

Belt

Hands

Animal-skin loincloth

Carvings mark the pillars as stylized human figures, but did they represent powerful people or supernatural beings?

A pillar's shape was refined before being carved and placed.

Pillars
Excavated
Unexcavated
Area shown in illustration

Entry pillars

— 159 ft —

Sanctuary grounds
Geomagnetic surveys of the 22-acre site suggest that at least 20 temples were built, from about 9600 to 8200 B.C. The oldest known are shown above.

Quarrying a pillar
The T-shape was incised directly into a bed of limestone. Pressure applied with levers then broke the rock along natural fracture lines, freeing the pillar.

Human muscle moved the limestone pillars, weighing up to 16 tons, from quarries as far as a quarter mile away.

The inner ring had no door and may have been accessed with ladders. Animal pelts may have hung on the pillars as offerings.

Offerings

Children may have helped by hauling rainwater collected in cisterns for drinking.

A sunken U-shaped block formed the entry pillars.

Spectator access? Earthen embankments may have given pilgrims a view of ceremonies inside the rings. Or the temple may have been roofed and exclusive.

Possible roof

FERNANDO G. BAPTISTA (ART) AND LAWSON PARKER (MAP AND DIAGRAMS), NGM STAFF; PATRICIA HEALY

SOURCES: KLAUS SCHMIDT, JENS NOTROFF, AND OLIVER DIETRICH, GERMAN ARCHAEOLOGICAL INSTITUTE; IAN KUIJT, UNIVERSITY OF NOTRE DAME

In southeastern Turkey some villagers still harvest wheat with a sickle. Einkorn wheat was first domesticated here, perhaps to feed the crowds who came to worship at Göbekli Tepe.

(Continued from page 35) littered with the greatest store of ancient flint tools Schmidt had ever seen—a Neolithic warehouse of knives, choppers, and projectile points. Even though the stone had to be lugged from neighboring valleys, Schmidt says, "there were more flints in one little area here, a square meter or two, than many archaeologists find in entire sites."

The circles follow a common design. All are made from limestone pillars shaped like giant spikes or capital T's. Bladelike, the pillars are easily five times as wide as they are deep. They stand an arm span or more apart, interconnected by low stone walls. In the middle of each ring are two taller pillars, their thin ends mounted in shallow grooves cut into the floor. I asked German architect and civil engineer Eduard Knoll, who works with Schmidt to preserve the site, how well designed the mounting system was for the central pillars. "Not," he said, shaking his head. "They hadn't yet mastered engineering." Knoll speculated that the pillars may have been propped up, perhaps by wooden posts.

To Schmidt, the T-shaped pillars are stylized human beings, an idea bolstered by the carved arms that angle from the "shoulders" of some pillars, hands reaching toward their loincloth-draped bellies. The stones face the center of the circle—as at "a meeting or dance," Schmidt says—a representation, perhaps, of a religious ritual. As for the prancing, leaping animals on the figures, he noted that they are mostly deadly creatures: stinging scorpions, charging boars, ferocious lions. The figures represented by the pillars may be guarded by them, or appeasing them, or incorporating them as totems.

Puzzle piled upon puzzle as the excavation continued. For reasons yet unknown, the rings at Göbekli Tepe seem to have regularly lost their power, or at least their charm. Every few decades people buried the pillars and put up new stones—a second, smaller ring, inside the first. Sometimes, later, they installed a third. Then the whole assemblage would be filled in with debris, and an entirely new circle created nearby. The site may have been built, filled in, and built again for centuries.

Bewilderingly, the people at Göbekli Tepe got steadily worse at temple building. The earliest rings are the biggest and most sophisticated, technically and artistically. As time went by, the pillars became smaller, simpler, and were mounted with less and less care. Finally the effort seems to have petered out altogether by 8200 B.C. Göbekli Tepe was all fall and no rise.

As important as what the researchers found was what they did not find: any sign of habitation. Hundreds of people must have been required to carve and erect the pillars, but the site had no water source—the nearest stream was about three miles away. Those workers would have needed homes, but excavations have uncovered no sign of walls, hearths, or houses—no other buildings that Schmidt has

Göbekli Totems

Animals carved on pillars at the site are native to the area and may represent guardian spirits.

Boar   Crane   Fox   Scorpion   Snakes

SOURCE: LAWSON PARKER, NGM STAFF.

interpreted as domestic. They would have had to be fed, but there is also no trace of agriculture. For that matter, Schmidt has found no mess kitchens or cooking fires. It was purely a ceremonial center. If anyone ever lived at this site, they were less its residents than its staff. To judge by the thousands of gazelle and aurochs bones found at the site, the workers seem to have been fed by constant shipments of game, brought from faraway hunts. All of this complex endeavor must have had organizers and overseers, but there is as yet no good evidence of a social hierarchy—no living area reserved for richer people, no tombs filled with elite goods, no sign of some people having better diets than others.

"These people were foragers," Schmidt says, people who gathered plants and hunted wild animals. "Our picture of foragers was always just small, mobile groups, a few dozen people. They cannot make big permanent structures, we thought, because they must move around to follow the resources. They can't maintain a separate class of priests and craft workers, because they can't carry around all the extra supplies to feed them. Then here is Göbekli Tepe, and they obviously did that."

Discovering that hunter-gatherers had constructed Göbekli Tepe was like finding that someone had built a 747 in a basement with an X-Acto knife. "I, my colleagues, we all thought, What? How?" Schmidt said. Paradoxically, Göbekli Tepe appeared to be both a harbinger of the civilized world that was to come and the last, greatest emblem of a nomadic past that was already disappearing. The accomplishment was astonishing, but it was hard to understand how it had been done or what it meant. "In 10 or 15 years," Schmidt predicts, "Göbekli Tepe

Discovering that Hunter-gatherers had constructed Göbekli Tepe was like finding that someone had built a 747 in a basement with an X-Acto Knife.

will be more famous than Stonehenge. And for good reason."

Hovering over Göbekli Tepe is the ghost of V. Gordon Childe. An Australian transplant to Britain, Childe was a flamboyant man, a passionate Marxist who wore plus fours and bow ties and larded his public addresses with noodle-headed paeans to Stalinism. He was also one of the most influential archaeologists of the past century. A great synthesist, Childe wove together his colleagues' disconnected facts into overarching intellectual schemes. The most famous of these arose in the 1920s, when he invented the concept of the Neolithic Revolution.

In today's terms, Childe's views could be summed up like this: Homo sapiens burst onto the scene about 200,000 years ago. For most of the millennia that followed, the species changed remarkably little, with humans living as small bands of wandering foragers. Then came the Neolithic Revolution—"a radical change," Childe said, "fraught with revolutionary consequences for the whole species." In a lightning bolt of inspiration, one part of humankind turned its back on foraging and embraced agriculture. The adoption of farming, Childe argued, brought with it further transformations. To tend their fields, people had to stop wandering and move into permanent villages, where they developed new tools and created pottery. The Neolithic Revolution, in his view, was an explosively important event—"the greatest in human history after the mastery of fire."

Of all the aspects of the revolution, agriculture was the most important. For thousands of years men and women with stone implements had wandered the landscape, cutting off heads of wild grain and taking them home. Even though these people may have tended and protected their *(Continued on page 47)*

On a limestone bowl from Nevalı Çori, a settlement founded a thousand years after Göbekli Tepe, two figures dance with an animal. Perhaps guides to the spirit realm, animals were important symbols when humans began domesticating sheep, goats, and other beasts.

Clues to what may have been the world's first organized religion are scattered throughout Neolithic sites in southern Turkey, northern Syria, and Iraq. The most common icons were the dangerous beasts hovering outside humankind's newly formed settlements, including boars (below, from Göbekli Tepe) and snakes (right, on the back of a human head from Nevalı Çori). Though images of humans are rare, one dating to at least 8000 B.C. (left), discovered nine miles from Göbekli Tepe, is the earliest known life-size sculpture.

(Continued from page 43) grain patches, the plants they watched over were still wild. Wild wheat and barley, unlike their domesticated versions, shatter when they are ripe—the kernels easily break off the plant and fall to the ground, making them next to impossible to harvest when fully ripe. Genetically speaking, true grain agriculture began only when people planted large new areas with mutated plants that did not shatter at maturity, creating fields of domesticated wheat and barley that, so to speak, waited for farmers to harvest them.

Rather than having to comb through the landscape for food, people could now grow as much as they needed and where they needed it, so they could live together in larger groups. Population soared. "It was only after the revolution—but immediately thereafter—that our species really began to multiply at all fast," Childe wrote. In these suddenly more populous societies, ideas could be more readily exchanged, and rates of technological and social innovation soared. Religion and art—the hallmarks of civilization—flourished.

Childe, like most researchers today, believed that the revolution first occurred in the Fertile Crescent, the arc of land that curves northeast from Gaza into southern Turkey and then sweeps southeast into Iraq. Bounded on the south by the harsh Syrian Desert and on the north by the mountains of Turkey, the crescent is a band of temperate climate between inhospitable extremes. Its eastern terminus is the confluence of the Tigris and Euphrates Rivers in southern Iraq—the site of a realm known as Sumer, which dates back to about 4000 B.C. In Childe's day most researchers agreed that Sumer represented the beginning of civilization. Archaeologist Samuel Noah Kramer summed up that view in the 1950s in his book History Begins at Sumer. Yet even before Kramer finished writing, the picture was being revised at the opposite, western end of the Fertile Crescent. In the Levant—the area that today encompasses Israel, the Palestinian territories, Lebanon, Jordan, and western Syria—archaeologists had discovered settlements dating as far back as 13,000 B.C. Known as Natufian villages (the name comes from the first of these sites to be found), they sprang up across the Levant as the Ice Age was drawing to a close, ushering in a time when the region's climate became relatively warm and wet.

The discovery of the Natufians was the first rock through the window of Childe's Neolithic Revolution. Childe had thought agriculture the necessary spark that led to villages and ignited civilization. Yet although the Natufians lived in permanent settlements of up to several hundred people, they were foragers, not farmers, hunting gazelles and gathering wild rye, barley, and wheat. "It was a big sign that our ideas needed to be revised," says Harvard University archaeologist Ofer Bar-Yosef.

Natufian villages ran into hard times around 10,800 B.C., when regional temperatures abruptly fell some 12°F, part of a mini ice age that lasted 1,200 years and created much drier conditions across the Fertile Crescent. With animal habitat and grain patches shrinking, a number of villages suddenly became too populous for the local food supply. Many people once again became wandering foragers, searching the landscape for remaining food sources.

Some settlements tried to adjust to the more arid conditions. The village of Abu Hureyra, in what is now northern Syria, seemingly tried to cultivate local stands of rye, perhaps replanting them. After examining rye grains from the site, Gordon Hillman of University College London and Andrew Moore of the Rochester Institute of Technology argued in 2000 that some were bigger than their wild equivalents—a possible sign of domestication, because cultivation inevitably increases qualities, such as fruit and seed size, that people find valuable. Bar-Yosef and some other researchers came to believe that nearby sites like Mureybet and Tell Qaramel also had agriculture. (Continued on page 50)

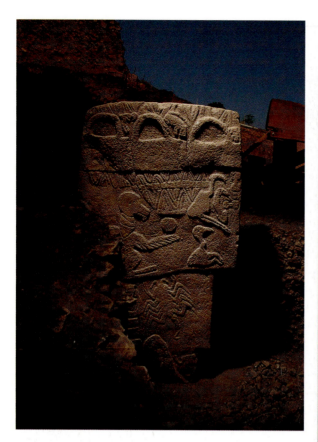

The elegant bas-reliefs of vultures, scorpions, and other creatures found on the T-shaped pillars had to have been created
by skilled artisans, evidence that hunter-gatherers were capable
of a complex social structure. Archaeologists have found a
partially quarried pillar (right) in the limestone hills around
Göbekli Tepe, which can be seen on the mound in the distance.

(Continued from page 47) If these archaeologists were correct, these protovillages provided a new explanation of how complex society began. Childe thought that agriculture came first, that it was the innovation that allowed humans to seize the opportunity of a rich new environment to extend their dominion over the natural world. The Natufian sites in the Levant suggested instead that settlement came first and that farming arose later, as a product of crisis. Confronted with a drying, cooling environment and growing populations, humans in the remaining fecund areas thought, as Bar-Yosef puts it, "If we move, these other folks will exploit our resources. The best way for us to survive is to settle down and exploit our own area." Agriculture followed.

The idea that the Neolithic Revolution was driven by climate change resonated during the 1990s, a time when people were increasingly worried about the effects of modern global warming. It was promoted in countless articles and books and ultimately enshrined in Wikipedia. Yet critics charged that the evidence was weak, not least because Abu Hureyra, Mureybet, and many other sites in northern Syria had been flooded by dams before they could be fully excavated. "You had an entire theory on the origins of human culture essentially based on a half a dozen unusually plump seeds," ancient-grain specialist George Willcox of the National Center for Scientific Research, in France, says. "Isn't it more likely that these grains were puffed during charring or that somebody at Abu Hureyra found some unusual-looking wild rye?"

As the dispute over the Natufians sharpened, Schmidt was carefully working at Göbekli Tepe. And what he was finding would, once again, force many researchers to reassess their ideas.

Anthropologists have assumed that organized religion began as a way of salving the tensions that inevitably arose when hunter-gatherers settled down, became farmers, and developed large societies. Compared to a nomadic band, the society of a village had longer term, more complex aims—storing grain and maintaining permanent homes. Villages would be more likely to accomplish those aims if their members were committed to the collective enterprise. Though primitive religious practices—burying the dead, creating cave art and figurines—had emerged tens of thousands of years earlier, organized religion arose, in this view, only when a common vision of a celestial order was needed to bind together these big, new, fragile groups of humankind. It could also have helped justify the social hierarchy that emerged in a more complex society: Those who rose to power were seen as having a special connection with the gods. Communities of the faithful, united in a common view of the world and their place in it, were more cohesive than ordinary clumps of quarreling people.

Göbekli Tepe, to Schmidt's way of thinking, suggests a reversal of that scenario: The construction of a massive temple by a group of foragers is evidence that organized religion could have come before the rise of agriculture and other aspects of civilization. It suggests that the human impulse to gather for sacred rituals arose as humans shifted from seeing themselves as part of the natural world to seeking mastery over it. When foragers began settling down in villages, they unavoidably created a divide between the human realm—a fixed huddle of homes with hundreds of inhabitants—and the dangerous land beyond the campfire, populated by lethal beasts.

French archaeologist Jacques Cauvin believed this change in consciousness was a "revolution of symbols," a conceptual shift that allowed humans to imagine gods—supernatural beings resembling humans—that existed in a universe beyond the physical world. Schmidt sees Göbekli Tepe as evidence for Cauvin's theory. "The animals were guardians to the spirit world," he says. "The reliefs on the T-shaped pillars illustrate that other world."

Schmidt speculates that foragers living within a hundred-mile radius of Göbekli Tepe created the temple as a holy place to gather and meet, perhaps bringing gifts and tributes to its priests and craftspeople. Some kind of social organization would have been necessary not only to build it but also to deal with the crowds it attracted. One imagines chanting and drumming, the animals on the great pillars seeming to move in flickering torchlight. Surely there were feasts; Schmidt has uncovered stone basins that could have been used for beer. The temple was a spiritual locus, but it may also have been the Neolithic version of Disneyland.

Over time, Schmidt believes, the need to acquire sufficient food for those who worked and gathered for ceremonies at Göbekli Tepe may have led to the intensive cultivation of wild cereals and the creation of some of the first domestic strains. Indeed, scientists now believe that one center of agriculture arose in southern Turkey—well within trekking distance of Göbekli Tepe—at exactly the time the temple was at its height. Today the closest known wild ancestors of modern einkorn wheat are found on the slopes of Karaca Dağ, a mountain just 60 miles northeast of Göbekli Tepe. In other words, the turn to agriculture celebrated by V. Gordon Childe may have been the result of a need that runs deep in the human psyche, a hunger that still moves people today to travel the globe in search of awe-inspiring sights.

Some of the first evidence for plant domestication comes from Nevalı Çori (pronounced nuh-vah-LUH CHO-ree), a settlement in the mountains scarcely 20 miles

> **G**öbekli Tepe may have been **a holy place for people to gather.** It may also have been the Neolithic version of Disneyland.

away. Like Göbekli Tepe, Nevalı Çori came into existence right after the mini ice age, a time archaeologists describe with the unlovely term Pre-pottery Neolithic (PPN). Nevalı Çori is now inundated by a recently created lake that provides electricity and irrigation water for the region. But before the waters shut down research, archaeologists found T-shaped pillars and animal images much like those Schmidt would later uncover at Göbekli Tepe. Similar pillars and images occurred in PPN settlements up to a hundred miles from Göbekli Tepe. Much as one can surmise today that homes with images of the Virgin Mary belong to Christians, Schmidt says, the imagery in these PPN sites indicates a shared religion—a community of faith that surrounded Göbekli Tepe and may have been the world's first truly large religious grouping.

Naturally, some of Schmidt's colleagues disagree with his ideas. The lack of evidence of houses, for instance, doesn't prove that nobody lived at Göbekli Tepe. And increasingly, archaeologists studying the origins of civilization in the Fertile Crescent are suspicious of any attempt to find a one-size-fits-all scenario, to single out one primary trigger. It is more as if the occupants of various archaeological sites were all playing with the building blocks of civilization, looking for combinations that worked. In one place agriculture may have been the foundation; in another, art and religion; and over there, population pressures or social organization and hierarchy. Eventually they all ended up in the same place. Perhaps there is no single path to civilization; instead it was arrived at by different means in different places.

In Schmidt's view, many of his colleagues have been as slow to appreciate Göbekli Tepe

as he has been to excavate it. This summer will mark his 17th year at the site. The annals of archaeology are replete with scientists who in their hurry carelessly wrecked important finds, losing knowledge for all time. Schmidt is determined not to add his name to the list. Today less than a tenth of the 22-acre site is open to the sky.

Schmidt emphasizes that further research on Göbekli Tepe may change his current understanding of the site's importance. Even its age is not clear—Schmidt is not certain he has reached the bottom layer. "We come up with two new mysteries for every one that we solve," he says. Still, he has already drawn some conclusions. "Twenty years ago everyone believed civilization was driven by ecological forces," Schmidt says. "I think what we are learning is that civilization is a product of the human mind."

Discussion Questions:

- How are recent finds at Göbekli Tepe changing archaeologists' understanding of the relationship between agriculture, organized religion, and monumental constructions?

- According to the article, how was Göbekli Tepe used, and by whom? Why is the existence of Göbekli Tepe described as being as surprising as "finding that someone had built a 747 in a basement with an X-Acto knife"?

Archaeological Interpretations:

- How are archaeologists reconstructing the ways in which Göbekli Tepe was being used and by whom? Do you think that these reconstructions are justified or are there other potential ways of interpreting the data? If there are other ways, what would they be?

- If the interpretation of Göbekli Tepe as being the world's first temple is correct, then how does this rewrite our understanding of how humanity shifted from relatively simple bands of hunter-gatherers to something more complex?

Paradigm Creation:
Material Primacy and the Power of Ideas within Religion

- How are the archaeological finds at Göbekli Tepe and Natufian villages challenging V. Gordon Childe's hypothesis regarding the Neolithic Revolution? Specifically, how might these finds suggest that the Neolithic Revolution might be less about ecological changes and more about ideological shifts?

- What do you think was the effect of religion on ancient cultures? How is it the same or different than in modern societies?

BEYOND THE BLUE HORIZON

By focusing on recent archaeological finds from Pacific islands, this article outlines our current understanding of how humans colonized this vast ocean. Evidence shows that these islands were colonized in two major waves of human movement. The first wave, around 800 B.C., was limited to the relatively near-by Melanesian Islands. More than a thousand years later, Polynesians launched a second wave as far as the distant islands of Easter Island, Hawaii, and New Zealand. How these colonizations occurred with relatively primitive sailing technologies is still poorly understood, as are the reasons for these long-distance journeys.

When reading this article, you should focus on:

- What is the timing of human colonization of the Pacific islands? How many waves of colonization were there and what are the names of the cultures who completed them?
- What might have prompted the colonization of the Pacific?
- How did the colonizers overcome the difficulties associated with long-distance seafaring?
- What environmental conditions might have been associated with Pacific colonization?

Its sails like fins against the dawn sky, the Hokule'a, a modern Hawaiian voyaging canoe built on ancient designs, glides into port after a 3,800-mile voyage.

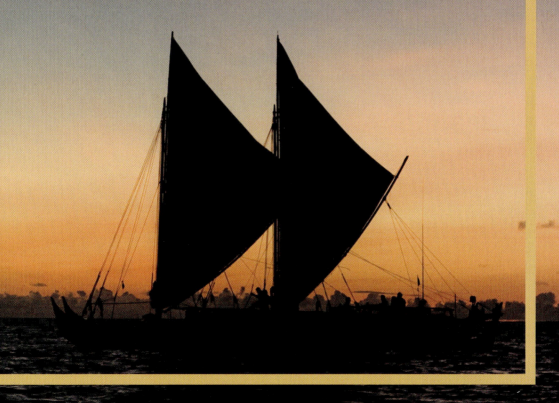

BEYOND THE BLUE HORIZON

By Roff Smith

Photographs by Stephen Alvarez

On Easter Island, also called Rapa Nui, mysterious statues stand sentinel as the Milky Way spins cold and bright above. The giant moai may represent ancestors who ruled here after Polynesians discovered the island some thousand years ago during a wave of exploration that has been compared in its boldness to modern space voyages.

THE FAR-FLUNG
ISLANDS OF THE PACIFIC

The discoveries there have also **opened a window** into the shadowy world of those early voyagers.

Much of the thrill of venturing to the far side of the world rests on the romance of difference. So one feels a certain sympathy for Captain James Cook on the day in 1778 that he "discovered" Hawaii. Then on his third expedition to the Pacific, the British navigator had explored scores of islands across the breadth of the sea, from lush New Zealand to the lonely wastes of Easter Island. This latest voyage had taken him thousands of miles north from the Society Islands to an archipelago so remote that even the old Polynesians back on Tahiti knew nothing about it. Imagine Cook's surprise, then, when the natives of Hawaii came paddling out in their canoes and greeted him in a familiar tongue, one he had heard on virtually every mote of inhabited land he had visited. Marveling at the ubiquity of this Pacific language and culture, he later wondered in his journal: "How shall we account for this Nation spreading it self so far over this Vast ocean?"

That question, and others that flow from it, has tantalized inquiring minds for centuries: Who were these amazing seafarers? Where did they come from, starting more than 3,000 years ago? And how could a Neolithic people with simple canoes and no navigation gear manage to find, let alone colonize, hundreds of far-flung island specks scattered across an ocean that spans nearly a third of the globe?

Answers have been slow in coming. But now a startling archaeological find on the island of Éfaté, in the Pacific nation of Vanuatu, has revealed an ancient seafaring people, the distant ancestors of today's Polynesians, taking their first steps into the unknown. The discoveries there have also opened a window into the shadowy world of those early voyagers.

At the same time, other pieces of this human puzzle are turning up in unlikely places. Climate data gleaned from slow-growing corals around the Pacific and from sediments in alpine lakes in South America may help explain how, more than a thousand years later, a second wave of seafarers beat their way across the entire Pacific.

Adapted from "Beyond the Blue Horizon" by Roff Martin Smith: National Geographic Magazine, March 2008.

Carvings believed to depict canoe sails scar volcanic stone at the Kona Village Resort on Hawaii, which may once have been the site of a navigators' school. Researchers have studied these and other carvings for clues about ancient Polynesian technology.

On a lonely sun-drenched knoll on Éfaté, about half an hour's drive east of Port-Vila, the old colonial capital of Vanuatu, Matthew Spriggs is sitting on an upturned bucket, gently brushing away crumbs of dirt from a richly decorated piece of pottery unearthed only a few minutes earlier. "I've never seen anything like this," he says, admiring the intricate design. "Nobody has. This is unique."

That description fits much of what is coming out of the ground here. "What we have is a first- or second-generation site containing the graves of some of the Pacific's first explorers," says Spriggs, professor of archaeology at the Australian National University and co-leader of an international team excavating the site. It came to light only by luck. A backhoe operator, digging up topsoil on the grounds of a derelict coconut plantation, scraped open a grave— the first of dozens in a burial ground some 3,000 years old. It is the oldest cemetery ever found in the Pacific islands, and it harbors the bones of an ancient people archaeologists call the Lapita, a label that derives from a beach in New Caledonia where a landmark cache of their pottery was found in the 1950s.

They were daring blue-water adventurers who roved the sea not just as explorers but also as pioneers, bringing along everything they would need to build new lives—their families and livestock, taro seedlings and stone tools. Within the span of a few centuries the Lapita stretched the boundaries of their world from the jungle-clad volcanoes of Papua New Guinea to the loneliest coral outliers of Tonga, at least 2,000 miles eastward in the Pacific. Along the way they explored millions of square miles of unknown sea, discovering and colonizing scores of tropical islands never before seen by human eyes: Vanuatu, New Caledonia, Fiji, Samoa.

It was their descendants, centuries later, who became the great Polynesian navigators we all tend to think of: the Tahitians and Hawaiians, the New Zealand Maori, and the curious people who erected those statues on Easter Island. But it was the Lapita who laid the foundation—who bequeathed to the islands the language, customs, and cultures that their more famous descendants carried around the Pacific.

While the Lapita left a glorious legacy, they also left precious few clues about themselves. What little is known or surmised about them has been pieced together from fragments of pottery, animal bones, obsidian flakes, and such oblique sources as comparative linguistics and geochemistry. Although their voyages can be traced back to the northern islands of Papua New Guinea, their language—variants of which are still spoken across the Pacific—came from Taiwan. And their peculiar style of pottery decoration, created by pressing a carved stamp into the clay, probably had its roots in the northern Philippines.

With the discovery of the Lapita cemetery on Éfaté, the volume of data available to researchers has expanded dramatically. The bones of at least 62 individuals have been uncovered so far—including old men, young women, even babies—and more skeletons are known to be in the ground.

Archaeologists were also thrilled to discover six complete Lapita pots; before this, only four had ever been found. Other discoveries included a burial urn with modeled birds arranged on the rim as though peering down at the human bones sealed inside. It's an important find, Spriggs says, for it conclusively identifies the remains as Lapita. "It would be hard for anyone to argue that these aren't Lapita when you have human bones enshrined inside what is unmistakably a Lapita urn."

Several lines of evidence also undergird Spriggs's conclusion that this was a community of pioneers making their first voyages into the remote reaches of Oceania. For one thing, the radiocarbon dating of bones and charcoal places them early in the Lapita expansion. For another, the chemical makeup of the obsidian flakes littering the site indicates that the rock wasn't local; instead it was imported from a large island in Papua New Guinea's Bismarck Archipelago, the springboard for the Lapita's thrust into the Pacific. This beautiful volcanic glass was fashioned into cutting and scraping tools, exactly the type of survival gear explorers would have packed into their canoes.

A particularly intriguing clue comes from chemical tests on the teeth of several skeletons. Then as now, the food and water you consume as a child deposits oxygen, carbon, strontium, and other elements in your still-forming adult teeth. The isotope signatures of these elements vary subtly from place to place, so that if you grow up in, say, Buffalo, New York, then spend your adult life in California, tests on the isotopes in your teeth will always reveal your eastern roots.

Isotope analysis indicates that several of the Lapita buried on Éfaté didn't spend their childhoods here but came from somewhere else. And while isotopes can't pinpoint their precise island of origin, this much is clear: At some point in their lives, these people left the villages of their birth and made a voyage by seagoing canoe, never to return.

DNA teased from these ancient bones may also help answer one of the most puzzling questions in Pacific anthropology: Did all Pacific islanders spring from one source or many? Was there only one outward migration from a single point in Asia, or several from different points? "This represents the best opportunity we've had yet," says Spriggs, "to find out who the Lapita actually were, where they came from, and who their closest descendants are today."

There is one stubborn question for which archaeology has yet to provide any answers: How did the Lapita accomplish the ancient equivalent of a moon landing, many times over? No one has found one of their canoes or any rigging, which could reveal how the canoes were sailed. Nor do the oral histories and traditions of later Polynesians offer (Continued on page 62)

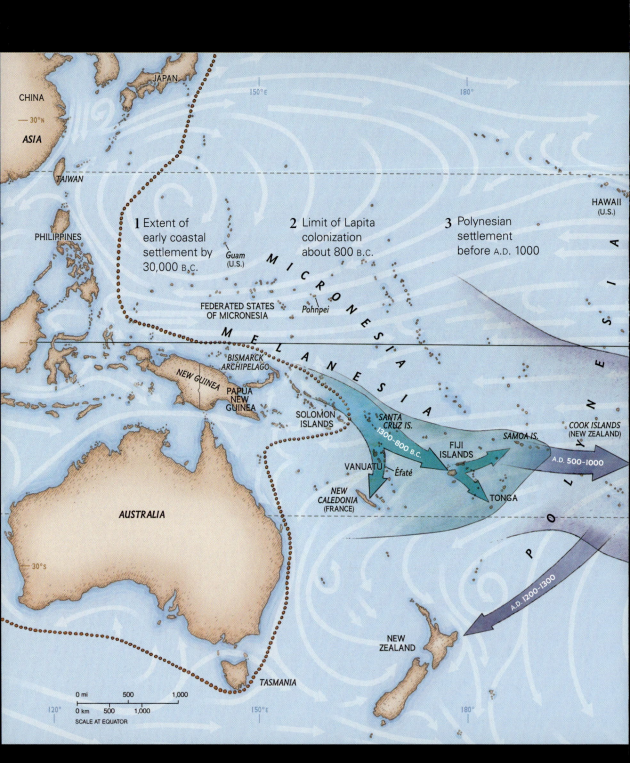

1 Extent of early coastal settlement by 30,000 B.C.

2 Limit of Lapita colonization about 800 B.C.

3 Polynesian settlement before A.D. 1000

CHINA

ASIA

30°N

TAIWAN

JAPAN

PHILIPPINES

150°E

180°

HAWAII (U.S.)

Guam (U.S.)

M I C R O N E S I A

FEDERATED STATES OF MICRONESIA

Pohnpei

M E L A N E S I A

BISMARCK ARCHIPELAGO

NEW GUINEA

PAPUA NEW GUINEA

SOLOMON ISLANDS

SANTA CRUZ IS. 1300-800 B.C.

VANUATU

Éfaté

NEW CALEDONIA (FRANCE)

FIJI ISLANDS

SAMOA IS.

TONGA

COOK ISLANDS (NEW ZEALAND)

P O L Y N E S I A

A.D. 500-1000

A.D. 1200-1300

AUSTRALIA

30°S

TASMANIA

NEW ZEALAND

120°

150°E

180°

0 mi   500   1,000

0 km   500   1,000

SCALE AT EQUATOR

FANTASTIC VOYAGE

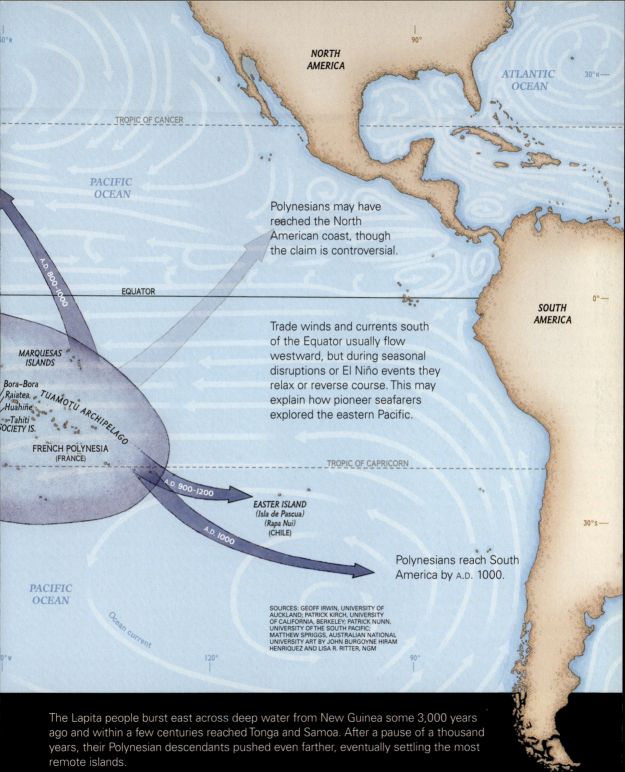

NORTH
AMERICA

ATLANTIC
OCEAN

30°N

90°

50°W

TROPIC OF CANCER

PACIFIC
OCEAN

Polynesians may have
reached the North
American coast, though
the claim is controversial.

A.D. 800-1000

EQUATOR

0°

SOUTH
AMERICA

MARQUESAS
ISLANDS

Bora-Bora
Raiatea
Huahiñe
Tahiti
SOCIETY IS.

TUAMOTU ARCHIPELAGO

FRENCH POLYNESIA
(FRANCE)

Trade winds and currents south
of the Equator usually flow
westward, but during seasonal
disruptions or El Niño events they
relax or reverse course. This may
explain how pioneer seafarers
explored the eastern Pacific.

TROPIC OF CAPRICORN

A.D. 900-1200

EASTER ISLAND
(Isla de Pascua)
(Rapa Nui)
(CHILE)

A.D. 1000

Polynesians reach South
America by A.D. 1000.

30°S

PACIFIC
OCEAN

Ocean current

120°

90°

SOURCES: GEOFF IRWIN, UNIVERSITY OF
AUCKLAND; PATRICK KIRCH, UNIVERSITY
OF CALIFORNIA, BERKELEY; PATRICK NUNN,
UNIVERSITY OF THE SOUTH PACIFIC;
MATTHEW SPRIGGS, AUSTRALIAN NATIONAL
UNIVERSITY ART BY JOHN BURGOYNE HIRAM
HENRIQUEZ AND LISA R. RITTER, NGM

The Lapita people burst east across deep water from New Guinea some 3,000 years
ago and within a few centuries reached Tonga and Samoa. After a pause of a thousand
years, their Polynesian descendants pushed even farther, eventually settling the most
remote islands.

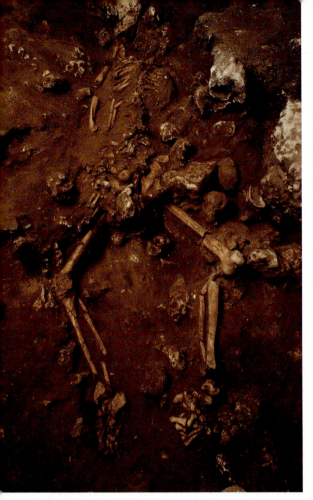

SECRETS OF THE LAPITA

Before 2004 few Lapita burial sites had been found. Then a backhoe operator on Éfaté island in Vanuatu accidentally discovered a cemetery containing at least 62 individuals. "We're seeing things we've never seen before," says archaeologist Stuart Bedford. The 3,000-year-old site is yielding details about these early explorers' distinctive ceramics, which bear stamped patterns (above), and their funeral rituals. No skulls were found with skeletons (left), some of which were also missing arm and rib bones. Evidence suggests the bones were removed after the bodies had decomposed. "The living knew who was buried there, and they were revisiting them," says Bedford. "It shows a very different attitude toward death."

(Continued from page 59) any insights, for they segue into myth long before they reach as far back in time as the Lapita.

"All we can say for certain is that the Lapita had canoes that were capable of ocean voyages, and they had the ability to sail them," says Geoff Irwin, a professor of archaeology at the University of Auckland and an avid yachtsman. Those sailing skills, he says, were developed and passed down over thousands of years by earlier mariners who worked their way through the archipelagoes of the western Pacific making short crossings to islands within sight of each other. The real adventure didn't begin, however, until their Lapita descendants neared the end of the Solomons chain, for this was the edge of the world. The nearest landfall, the Santa Cruz Islands, is almost 230 miles away, and for at least 150 of those miles the Lapita sailors would have been out of sight of land, with empty horizons on every side.

Yet that passage, around 1200 b.c., was just the warm-up act, for Santa Cruz and Vanuatu were the Lapita's first and easiest discoveries. Reaching Fiji, as they did a century or so later, meant crossing more than 500 miles of ocean, pressing on day after day into the great blue void of the Pacific. What gave them the courage to launch out on such a risky voyage?

The Lapita's thrust into the Pacific was eastward, against the prevailing trade winds, Irwin notes. Those nagging headwinds, he argues, may have been the key to their success. "They could sail out for days into the unknown and reconnoiter, secure in the knowledge that if they didn't find anything, they could turn about and catch a swift ride home on the trade winds. It's what made the whole thing work."

Once out there, skilled seafarers would detect abundant leads to follow to land: seabirds and turtles, coconuts and twigs carried out to sea by the tides, and the afternoon pileup of clouds

The Ocean boils as lava oozes into the waves at Hawai'i Volcanoes National Park. Scanning the horizon, Lapita and later Polynesian explorers may have used billowing columns of steam and ash from volcanic eruptions as navigation aids, steering for the promise of new land.

on the horizon that often betokens an island in the distance.

Some islands may have broadcast their presence with far less subtlety than a cloud bank. Some of the most violent eruptions anywhere on the planet during the past 10,000 years occurred in Melanesia, which sits nervously in one of the most explosive volcanic regions on Earth. Even less spectacular eruptions would have sent plumes of smoke billowing into the stratosphere and rained ash for hundreds of miles. It's possible that the Lapita saw these signs of distant islands and later sailed off in their direction, knowing they would find land.

For returning explorers, successful or not, the geography of their own archipelagoes provided a safety net to keep them from overshooting their home ports and sailing off into eternity. Vanuatu, for example, stretches more than 500 miles in a northwest-southeast trend, its scores of intervisible islands forming a backstop for mariners riding the trade winds home.

All this presupposes one essential detail, says Atholl Anderson, professor of prehistory at the Australian National University and, like Irwin, a keen yachtsman: that the Lapita had mastered the advanced art of tacking into the wind. "And there's no proof that they could do any such thing," Anderson says. "There has been this assumption that they must have done so, and people have built canoes to re-create those early voyages based on that assumption. But nobody has any idea what their canoes looked like or how they were rigged."

However they did it, the Lapita spread themselves a third of the way across the Pacific, then called it quits for reasons known only to them. Ahead lay the vast emptiness of the central Pacific, and perhaps they were too thinly stretched to venture farther. They probably never numbered more than a few thousand in total, and in their rapid migration eastward they encountered hundreds of islands—more than 300 in Fiji alone. Supplied with such an embarrassment of riches, they could settle down and enjoy what for a time were Earth's last Edens.

"It would have been absolutely amazing to have seen this place back then," says Stuart Bedford, an archaeologist from the Australian National University and co-leader,

Point of departure, the island of Raiatea in French Polynesia was a staging area for ancient voyagers who discovered Hawaii and New Zealand. After provisioning their canoes, sailors embarked from the temple of Taputaputea, the spiritual center of their world.

along with Matthew Spriggs, of the excavation on Éfaté. "These islands were far richer in biodiversity in those days than they are today." By way of illustration, he picks up a trochus shell the size of a dinner plate that was exposed in a test trench only that morning. "The reefs then were covered with thousands of these, each one a meal in itself. The seas were teeming with fish, and huge flightless birds could be found in the rain forest, virtually tame since they had never seen a human being. The Lapita would have thought they'd stumbled onto paradise."

As indeed it was. But theirs is a story of paradise found and lost, for although the Lapita were a Neolithic people, they had a modern capacity for overexploiting natural resources. Within a short span of time—a couple of generations, no more—those huge trochus shells vanished from the archaeological record. The plump flightless birds followed suit, as did a species of terrestrial crocodile. In all, it's estimated that more than a thousand species became extinct across the breadth of the Pacific islands after humans appeared on the scene.

Still, more than a millennium would pass before the Lapita's descendants, a people we now call the Polynesians, struck out in search of new territory. The pioneers who launched this second age of discovery some 1,200 or more years ago faced even greater challenges than their Lapita ancestors, for now they were sailing out beyond the island-stippled waters of Melanesia and western Polynesia and into the central Pacific, where distances are reckoned in thousands of miles, and tiny motes of islands are few and far between.

How difficult would it have been to find terra firma in all that watery wilderness? Consider this: When Magellan's fleet traversed the Pacific in 1520-21, sailing blind across an unknown sea, they went nearly four months without setting foot on land. (They missed the Society Islands, the Tuamotus, and the Marquesas, among other archipelagoes.) Many of the hapless sailors died of thirst, malnutrition, scurvy, and other diseases before the fleet reached the Philippines.

The early Polynesians found nearly everything there was to find, although it took them centuries to do so. Their feats of exploration are remembered and celebrated today at cultural festivals across the Pacific.

It is midafternoon, and a carnival atmosphere has settled over the beach at Matira Point on the island of Bora-Bora in French Polynesia. The air is fragrant with barbecue, and thousands of cheering spectators throng the shore to witness the grand finale of the Hawaiki Nui Va'a, a grueling, three-stage, 80-mile outrigger canoe race that virtually stops the nation.

"This is our heritage," says Manutea Owen, a former champion and a revered hero on his home island of Huahine. "Our people came from over the sea by canoe. Sometimes when I'm out there competing, I try to imagine what they must have endured and the adventures they had crossing those huge distances."

Imagination is now the only way one can conjure up those epic sea voyages. Like their Lapita ancestors, the earliest Polynesians left scanty artifacts of their seafaring life. Only a few pieces of one ancient canoe have ever been found, on Huahine in 1977. No surviving example of the great seagoing, sailing canoes thought to have borne the Polynesian pioneers has yet been discovered.

European explorers left the earliest descriptions of watercraft used by Pacific islanders. In the less isolated waters of Micronesia, they encountered sleek, lateen-rigged canoes, a style that may have filtered into the Pacific from China and the Arab world. But in the remote corners of Polynesia—Hawaii, the Marquesas, and New Zealand—the explorers saw only simple craft. Atholl Anderson suspects that these were the truly indigenous boats, the kind that, centuries earlier, carried Polynesian settlers to far islands.

Anderson also questions conventional wisdom about Polynesian seamanship, citing a later explorer, Captain Cook. While Cook was impressed with the speed of the Polynesian canoes—they could literally sail circles around his ships—he came to question the islanders' ability to make long, intentional sea voyages. He records an account of a group of Tahitians who, helpless in the face of a contrary wind and

STILTS AND STONE

From the simple stilt houses of the early Lapita to the giant moai of Easter Island, Pacific islanders developed a range of architectural and artistic styles. One of the most mysterious and massive examples is Nan Madol, seat of an ancient dynasty on the island of Pohnpei in Micronesia. Beginning about a.d. 500 and continuing for perhaps a thousand years, Pohnpeians built nearly a hundred artificial islets atop a flat expanse of reef. On these foundations they erected houses, ceremonial buildings, and robust tombs from thick columns of basalt. With its islets interspersed by canals, Nan Madol has been called the Venice of the Pacific.

unable to set a course for home, drifted hundreds of miles off course and were marooned on Aitutaki, in what is now the Cook Islands.

Rather than give all the credit to human skill and daring, Anderson invokes the winds of chance. El Niño, the same climate disruption that affects the Pacific today, may have helped scatter the first settlers to the ends of the ocean, Anderson suggests. Climate data obtained from slow-growing corals around the Pacific and from lake-bed sediments in the Andes of South America point to a series of unusually frequent El Niños around the time of the Lapita expansion, and again between 1,600 and 1,200 years ago, when the second *(Continued on page 68)*

*Imposing walls of a tomb complex on Pohnpei were built for
Nan Madol's rulers around a.d. 1350. Workers did not carve
the stone but chose natural basalt columns—some weighing
more than ten tons—and fit them expertly together.*

A late stop in the Polynesians' epic journey across Earth's greatest ocean, Easter Island wasn't necessarily their final destination. Evidence suggests that later explorers reached South America a few centuries before the arrival of another set of immigrants: Europeans.

(Continued from page 65) wave of pioneer navigators made their voyages farther east, to the remotest corners of the Pacific. By reversing the regular east-to-west flow of the trade winds for weeks at a time, these "super El Niños" might have sped the Pacific's ancient mariners on long, unplanned voyages far over the horizon.

The volley of El Niños that coincided with the second wave of voyages could have been key to launching Polynesians across the wide expanse of open water between Tonga, where the Lapita stopped, and the distant archipelagoes of eastern Polynesia. "Once they crossed that gap, they could island hop throughout the region, and from the Marquesas it's mostly downwind to Hawaii," Anderson says. It took another 400 years for mariners to reach Easter Island, which lies in the opposite direction—normally upwind. "Once again this was during a period of frequent El Niño activity."

Exactly how big a role El Niño played in dispersing humans across the Pacific is a matter of lively academic debate. Could lucky breaks and fickle winds really account for so wide a spread of people throughout the 65-million-square-mile vastness of the Pacific? By the time Europeans came on the scene, virtually every speck of habitable land, hundreds of islands and atolls in all, had already been discovered by native seafarers—who ultimately made it all the way to South America. Archaeologists in Chile recently found ancient chicken bones containing DNA that matches early Polynesian fowl.

Nor did they arrive as lone castaways who soon died out. They came to stay, in groups, with animals and crops from their former homes. "My sense is that there had to be something more at work here than canoes simply blown before a wind," says Irwin. He notes that the trade winds slacken during the summer monsoon, which might have allowed islanders to purposefully sail eastward. Moreover, says Irwin, "Sophisticated traditions of seafaring were planted in every island. Did they develop independently in all of those islands? If so, why do these traditions bear so many details in common?

"But whatever you believe, the really fascinating part of this story isn't the methods they used, but their motives. The Lapita, for example, didn't need to pick up and go; there was nothing forcing them, no overcrowded homeland.

"They went," he says, "because they wanted to go and see what was over the horizon."

Discussion Questions:

- What drives colonization of vastly dispersed areas like the Pacific islands?
- What are the names of the two primary groups that colonized the Pacific and how does the archaeological site of Éfaté fit into the story?
- What were the effects of human colonization on island ecosystems?

Archaeological Interpretations:

- How did the archaeologists working at Éfaté determine the original homeland of ancient skeletons that they uncovered? How did they determine the time period and cultural affiliation of these remains? Why was this considered important?
- What are some of the theories proposed within the article about how people were able to colonize the islands of the Pacific with relatively basic marine technology?

- How does the archaeological evidence of human colonization of the Pacific influence our ideas of human ingenuity and exploration?

Paradigm Creation:
Geographic Happenstance and Directed Human Action

- What are the supporting arguments for how and why people may have "accidentally" discovered and colonized the islands of the Pacific? What are the supporting arguments for a more purposeful discovery?
- How can we compare the story of Pacific colonization to other stories of "discovery" such as Columbus' travel to the Americas or the exploration of space? How do political, social, and environmental circumstances factor into these stories? How does each touch on themes of adventure, goal-oriented action, and luck?

LOFTY AMBITIONS OF THE INCA

Lofty Ambitions of the Inca outlines the history of
the Inca empire, the organizational principles and
practices that allowed its expansion, and its eventual
destruction at the hands of invading Europeans. The
article highlights recent archaeological research that
has uncovered the pre-empire roots of this civilization
in the fertile Cusco Valley. While military might was
certainly an important factor in expanding the empire,
the article argues that much of the Inca success was
based on their ability to organize manpower and
resources.

When reading this article, you should focus on:
- What were the conditions that allowed the creation
  of the Inca empire?
- How is recent archaeological research in South
  America bringing to light new aspects of the Inca
  and their predecessors?
- How did the Inca treat their dead, particularly those
  that were once rulers?

At Museo Leymebamba, Chachapoyas, Peru

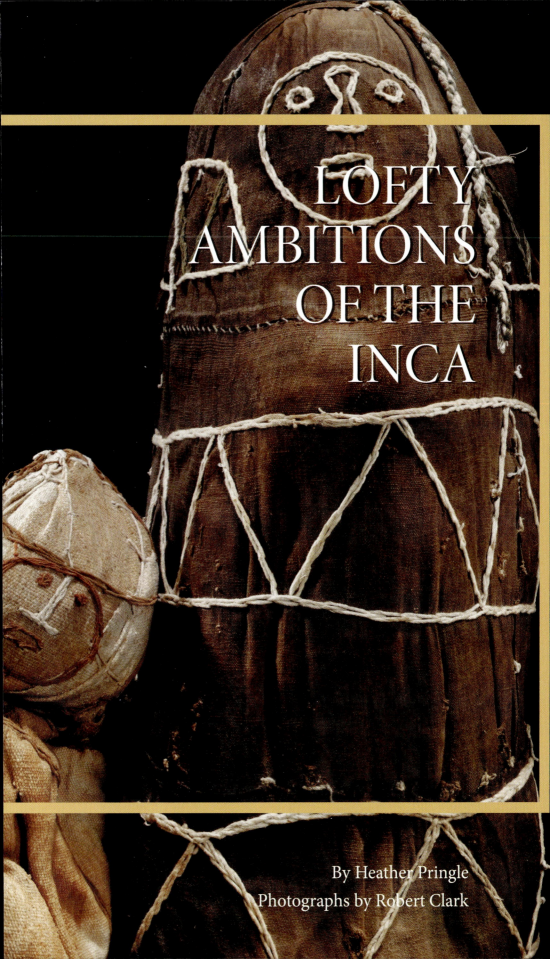

LOFTY
AMBITIONS
OF THE
INCA

By Heather Pringle
Photographs by Robert Clark

Perched high in the Peruvian Andes, the royal retreat of Machu Picchu testifies to the Inca's masterful building skills with its precision-cut stones and perfectly placed cascades of terraces.

At Lake Titicaca, craft vendors wait for tourists on an island sacred to the Inca. Far left: The small bundle is how the Chachapoya people kept their dead. The conquering Inca were inspired to make a similar bundle for the larger mummy.

Five centuries ago, these mummies were bound into bundles, which resulted in contorted poses but made them easier to carry. Modern looters tore off their wrappings, hoping to find gold.

Still standing after five and a half centuries of earthquakes, this stone wall in Ollantaytambo was once part of an estate owned by ruler Pachacutec Inca Yupanqui. The Inca had no iron tools or wheeled vehicles, yet they managed to quarry and move stones that weighed more than a hundred tons.

RISING
FROM OBSCURITY TO THE HEIGHTS OF POWER,
A SUCCESSION OF ANDEAN RULERS SUBDUED KINGDOMS, SCULPTED MOUNTAINS, AND FORGED A MIGHTY EMPIRE.

On the remote Peruvian island of Taquile, in the middle of the great Lake Titicaca, hundreds of people stand in silence on the plaza as a local Roman Catholic priest recites a prayer. Descended in part from Inca colonists sent here more than 500 years ago, the inhabitants of Taquile keep the old ways. They weave brilliantly colored cloth, speak the traditional language of the Inca, and tend their fields as they have for centuries. On festival days they gather in the plaza to dance to the sound of wooden pipes and drums.

Today, on a fine summer afternoon, I watch from the sidelines as they celebrate the fiesta of Santiago, or St. James. In Inca times this would have been the festival of Illapa, the Inca god of lightning. As the prayers draw to a close, four men dressed in black raise a rustic wooden litter holding a painted statue of Santiago. Walking behind the priest in a small procession, the bearers carry the saint for all in the plaza to see, just as the Inca once shouldered the mummies of their revered kings.

The names of those Inca rulers still resonate with power and ambition centuries after their demise: Viracocha Inca (meaning

Now archaeologists are making up for lost time.

Creator God Ruler), Huascar Inca (Golden Chain Ruler), and Pachacutec Inca Yupanqui (He Who Remakes the World). And remake the world they did. Rising from obscurity in Peru's Cusco Valley during the 13th century, a royal Inca dynasty charmed, bribed, intimidated, or conquered its rivals to create the largest pre-Columbian empire in the New World.

Scholars long possessed few clues about the lives of Inca kings, apart from flattering histories that Inca nobles told soon after the arrival of Spanish conquistadores. The Inca had no system of hieroglyphic writing, as the Maya did, and any portraits that Inca artists may have made of their rulers were lost. The royal palaces of Cusco, the Inca capital, fell swiftly to the European conquerors, and a new Spanish colonial city rose on their ruins, burying or obliterating the Inca past. In more recent times, civil unrest broke out in the Peruvian Andes in the early 1980s, and few archaeologists ventured into the Inca heartland for more than a decade.

Adapted from "Lofty Ambitions of the Inca " by Heather Pringle: National Geographic Magazine, April 2011.

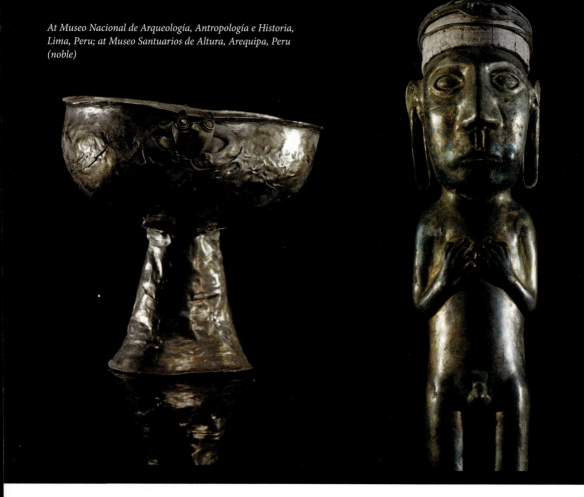

Now archaeologists are making up for lost time. Combing rugged mountain slopes near Cusco, they are discovering thousands of previously unknown sites, shedding new light on the origins of the Inca dynasty. Gleaning clues from colonial documents, they are relocating the lost estates of Inca rulers and examining the complex upstairs-and-downstairs lives of imperial households. And on the frontiers of the lost empire, they are piecing together dramatic evidence of the wars Inca kings fought and the psychological battles they waged to forge dozens of fractious ethnic groups into a united realm. Their extraordinary ability to triumph on the battlefield and to build a civilization, brick by brick, sent a clear message, says Dennis Ogburn, an archaeologist at the University of North Carolina at Charlotte: "I think they were saying, We are the most powerful people in the world, so don't even think of messing with us."

On a sun-washed July afternoon, Brian Bauer, an archaeologist from the University of Illinois at Chicago, stands in the plaza of the sprawling Inca ceremonial site of Maukallacta, south of Cusco. He takes a swig of water, then points to a towering outcrop of gray rock just to the east. Carved into its craggy summit are massive steps, part of a major Inca shrine. Some 500 years ago, says Bauer, pilgrims journeyed here to worship at the steep outcrop, once regarded as one of the most sacred places in the empire: the birthplace of the Inca dynasty.

Bauer, a wiry 54-year-old in a battered ball cap and blue jeans, first came to Maukallacta in the early 1980s to uncover the origins of the Inca Empire. At the time most historians and archaeologists believed that a brilliant, young Andean Alexander the Great named Pachacutec became the first Inca king in the early 1400s, transforming a small collection

of mud huts into a mighty empire in just one generation. Bauer didn't buy it. He believed the Inca dynasty had far deeper roots, and Maukallacta seemed the logical place to look for them. To his bewilderment, two field seasons of digging turned up no trace of primeval Inca lords.

So Bauer shifted north, to the Cusco Valley. With colleague R. Alan Covey, now an archaeologist at Southern Methodist University (SMU) in Dallas, and a team of Peruvian assistants, he marched up and down the steep mountain slopes in straight transect lines for four field seasons, recording every scattering of pottery sherds or toppled stone wall he came across. Persistence paid off. Bauer and his colleagues eventually discovered thousands of previously unknown Inca sites, and the new evidence revealed for the first time how an Inca state had risen much earlier than previously believed—sometime between 1200

and 1300. The ancient rulers of the region, the mighty Wari (Huari) lords who reigned from a capital near modern Ayacucho, had fallen by 1100, in part due to a severe drought that afflicted the Andes for a century or more. In the ensuing turmoil, local chiefs across the Peruvian highlands battled over scarce water and led raiders into neighboring villages in search of food. Hordes of refugees fled to frigid, windswept hideouts above 13,000 feet.

But in the fertile, well-watered valley around Cusco, Inca farmers stood their ground. Instead of splintering apart and warring among themselves, Inca villages united into a small state capable of mounting an organized defense. And between 1150 and 1300, the Inca around Cusco began to capitalize on a major warming trend in the Andes.

As temperatures climbed, Inca farmers moved up the slopes by *(Continued on page 86)*

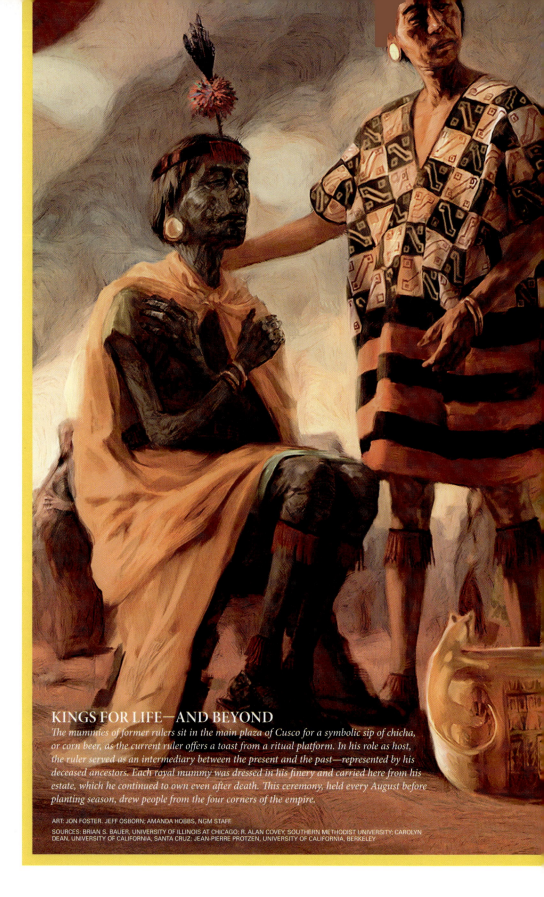

KINGS FOR LIFE—AND BEYOND

The mummies of former rulers sit in the main plaza of Cusco for a symbolic sip of chicha, or corn beer, as the current ruler offers a toast from a ritual platform. In his role as host, the ruler served as an intermediary between the present and the past—represented by his deceased ancestors. Each royal mummy was dressed in his finery and carried here from his estate, which he continued to own even after death. This ceremony, held every August before planting season, drew people from the four corners of the empire.

ART: JON FOSTER. JEFF OSBORN; AMANDA HOBBS, NGM STAFF.

SOURCES: BRIAN S. BAUER, UNIVERSITY OF ILLINOIS AT CHICAGO; R. ALAN COVEY, SOUTHERN METHODIST UNIVERSITY; CAROLYN DEAN, UNIVERSITY OF CALIFORNIA, SANTA CRUZ; JEAN-PIERRE PROTZEN, UNIVERSITY OF CALIFORNIA, BERKELEY

Former
Saphy
River

Modern
city blocks

Great
plaza

N̂

The great plaza of Cusco was the political center of the
Inca Empire. The Saphy River divided it into two sacred
spaces, with the northeast area used for ceremonies.

Ambition Unbound

After centuries as a growing local power, the Inca dreamed of a greater realm. They went on to conquer 300,000 square miles in a few generations.

1 ca 1400
Having subdued their neighbors, Inca kings launch their first conquests beyond the Cusco region.

2 ca 1470
Pushing to the coast, the Inca defeat the Chimú Empire and carry off many Chimú artisans.

3 ca 1500
Turning south, the Inca capture a vast territory, extending their reach to the edge of Patagonia.

4 by 1532
In a final thrust along the eastern slope of the Andes, the Inca expand farther into the Amazon Basin.

Sacred Valley detail at right →

THE INCA EMPIRE

Employing a shrewd combination of diplomacy, intermarriage, and military coercion, the Inca conquered a vast realm extending 2,500 miles along the mountainous spine of South America. At their height, they ruled as many as 12 million people, who spoke at least 20 languages. This fractious conglomeration quickly fell apart after the Spanish conquest in 1532.

Scale varies in this perspective. Distance from Lima to La Paz is 670 mi (1,078 km). Present-day place-names and boundaries shown.

WILLIAM E. McNULTY, LAWSON PARKER, AND LISA R. RITTER,
NGM STAFF. LANDSAT IMAGE (INSET): GLOBAL LAND COVER FACILITY

SOURCES: BRIAN S. BAUER, UNIVERSITY OF ILLINOIS AT CHICAGO;
R. ALAN COVEY, SOUTHERN METHODIST UNIVERSITY; TERENCE N. D'ALTROY,
COLUMBIA UNIVERSITY

VENEZUELA
GUYANA
SURINAME
COLOMBIA
AMAZON
Amazon
BASIN
SOUTH AMERICA
BRAZIL
Quito
ECUADOR
PERU
BOLIVIA
Cajamarca
Lima
Vilcabamba
Ayacucho
Maukallacta
Cusco
Lake Titicaca
La Paz
Sucre
PACIFIC OCEAN
ANDES
INCA ROAD
PARAGUAY
CHILE
ARGENTINA
Santiago
PATAGONIA

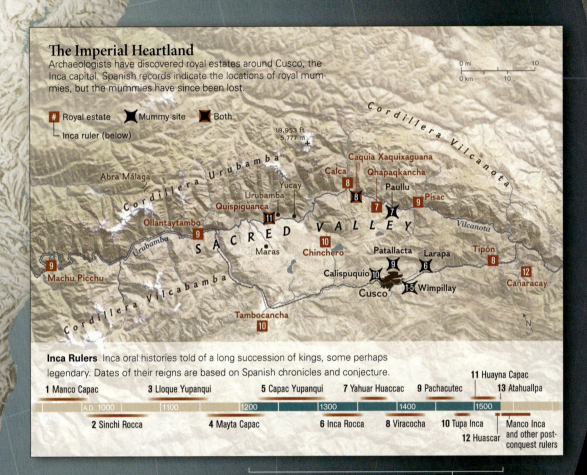

The Imperial Heartland

Archaeologists have discovered royal estates around Cusco, the Inca capital. Spanish records indicate the locations of royal mummies, but the mummies have since been lost.

0 mi — 10
0 km — 10

Royal estate ✕ Mummy site ◆ Both

Inca ruler (below)

ATLANTIC OCEAN

Cordillera Vilcanota

Cordillera Urubamba

Abra Málaga

18,953 ft
5,777 m

Caquia Xaquixaguana
Calca
Qhapaqkancha
8
8
Paullu
7 **7**
9 Pisac
Yucay
Urubamba
Quispiguanca **11**
Ollantaytambo
9
SACRED VALLEY
Vilcanota
Urubamba
Maras
Chinchero **10**
Patallacta
Larapa
Tipón
9 **6** **8**
Calispuquio
10 **15** Wimpillay
Cusco
12
Cañaracay
9
Machu Picchu
Cordillera Vilcabamba
Tambocancha
10

N

Inca Rulers Inca oral histories told of a long succession of kings, some perhaps legendary. Dates of their reigns are based on Spanish chronicles and conjecture.

| 1 Manco Capac | 3 Lloque Yupanqui | 5 Capac Yupanqui | 7 Yahuar Huaccac | 9 Pachacutec | 11 Huayna Capac |
| | | | | | 13 Atahuallpa |

A.D. 1000 — 1100 — 1200 — 1300 — 1400 — 1500

| 2 Sinchi Rocca | 4 Mayta Capac | 6 Inca Rocca | 8 Viracocha | 10 Tupa Inca | Manco Inca |
| | | | | 12 Huascar | and other post-conquest rulers |

The Late, Great Inca

Among the many native civilizations of the New World, the Inca developed relatively late but built the largest empire, unifying their diverse realm with an extensive road network.

South America — Mesoamerica — Inca

Wari
Tiwanaku
Nasca
Moche — Chimú
Teotihuacan — Aztec
Maya

A.D. 500 — 800 — 1100 — 1500

*Pre-Columbian cultural area that includes parts of present-day Mexico and Central America

A patchwork of farms covers land near Chinchero that likely belonged to the royal estate of Tupa Inca Yupanqui. The Inca expertly worked every agricultural niche in their vast territory. At this elevation, more than 12,000 feet, they grew tubers such as potatoes and herded domesticated llamas and alpacas.

(Continued from page 81) 800 to 1,000 feet, building tiers of agricultural terraces, irrigating their fields, and reaping record corn harvests. "These surpluses," says Alex Chepstow-Lusty, a paleoecologist at the French Institute for Andean Studies in Lima who has been studying the region's ancient climate, allowed the Inca to "free up many people for other roles, whether building roads or maintaining a large army." In time Inca rulers could call up more conscripts and supply a larger army than any neighboring chief.

With this big stick, Inca kings began eyeing the lands and resources of others. They struck marriage alliances with neighboring lords, taking their daughters as wives, and dispensed generous gifts to new allies. When a rival lord spurned their advances or stirred up trouble, they flexed their military might. In all the surrounding valleys, local lords succumbed one

by one, until there was only one mighty state and one capital, the sacred city of Cusco.

Flush with success, Inca kings set their sights farther afield, on the wealthy lands surrounding Lake Titicaca. Sometime after 1400, one of the greatest Inca rulers, Pachacutec Inca Yupanqui, began planning his conquest of the south. It was the dawn of empire.

Massed on a high, cold Peruvian plain north of the great lake in the mid-1400s, the army of the Colla bristled with battle gear, daring the Inca invaders to make war. Pachacutec scanned the enemy ranks in silence, preparing for the great battle ahead. The lords of the Titicaca region were haughty men, ruling as many as 400,000 people in kingdoms arrayed around the lake. Their lands were rich and desirable. Gold and silver veined the mountains, and herds of alpacas and llamas fattened in lush meadows. *(Continued on page 90)*

Women waiting for a lift at Abra Málaga wear clothing that reflects their country's history. Their shawls follow an Inca tradition, but their upturned hats and full skirts were inspired by the Spanish.

Under the care of a watchman, corn dries in the autumn air of Yucay. The Inca developed high-yield varieties of this grain that continue to thrive in the rich soil of the Urubamba River Valley. The empire's main crop, corn filled state granaries, fed laborers and soldiers, and was fermented into beer for festivals.

(Continued from page 87) Military success in the Andes depended on such livestock. A llama, the only draft animal on the continent, could carry 70 pounds of gear on its back. Llamas, along with alpacas, also provided meat, leather, and fiber for clothing. They were jeeps, K rations, and fatigues all rolled into one—crucial military assets. If the Inca king could not conquer the Titicaca lords who owned these vast herds, he would live in fear of the day these lords would come to conquer him.

Seated on a shimmering litter, Pachacutec issued the order to attack. Playing panpipes carved from the bones of enemies and war drums fashioned from the flayed skins of dead foes, his soldiers advanced toward the Colla forces, a moving wall of terror and intimidation. Then both sides charged. When the fog of battle lifted, Colla bodies littered the landscape.

In the years that followed, Pachacutec and his descendants subdued all the southern lords. "The conquest of the Titicaca Basin was the jewel in the crown of the Inca Empire," says Charles Stanish, an archaeologist at the University of California, Los Angeles. But military victory was only the first step in the Inca's grand strategy of empire building. Officials next set about establishing civil control.

If provinces mounted resistance, Inca sovereigns reshuffled their populations, deporting restive inhabitants to the Inca heartland and replacing them with loyal subjects. Residents of remote walled villages were moved to new Inca-controlled towns sited along Inca roads—roads that sped the movement of Inca troops. Inca governors ordered the construction of roadside storehouses for those troops and commanded local communities to fill them with provisions. "The Inca were the organizational geniuses of the Americas," says Stanish.

Under Inca rule, Andean civilization flowered as never before. Inca engineers transformed fragmentary road networks into interconnected highways. Inca farmers mastered high-altitude agriculture, cultivating some 70 different native crops and often stockpiling three to seven years' worth of food in vast storage complexes. Imperial officials excelled at the art of inventory control, tracking storehouse contents across the realm with an ancient Andean form of computer code—colored and knotted cords known as quipus. And Inca masons raised timeless architectural masterpieces like Machu Picchu, which continues to awe visitors today.

By the time the Inca king Huayna Capac took power around 1493, little seemed beyond the reach of the Inca dynasty. To bring grandeur to his new capital in Ecuador, Huayna Capac put more than 4,500 rebellious subjects to work hauling immense stone blocks all the way from Cusco—a distance of nearly a thousand miles up and down vertiginous mountain roads. And in the Inca heartland, a small army of men and women toiled to construct a royal estate for Huayna Capac and his family. At the king's bidding, they moved the Urubamba River to the southern side of the valley. They leveled hills and drained marshes, then planted corn and other crops such as cotton, peanuts, and hot peppers from far corners of the empire. In the center of the estate, they laid stones and bricks for Huayna Capac's new country palace, Quispiguanca.

As the late afternoon sun slants down, I wander the ruins of Quispiguanca with Alan Covey, the archaeologist from SMU. Situated on the outskirts of the modern town of Urubamba, Quispiguanca basks in one of the warmest and sunniest microclimates in the region, which provided the Inca royal family a welcome escape from the cold of Cusco. The estate's gatehouses now look out on a field of pungent cilantro, and its surviving walls enclose a royal compound that once sprawled over an area equivalent to some seven soccer fields.

Encircled by parkland, fields, and gardens, Quispiguanca was an Inca version of Camp David, a retreat from the world, a place for a

The Inca were the organizational geniuses of the Americas.

warrior-king to unwind after military campaigning. Here Huayna Capac entertained guests in the great halls and gambled with courtiers and other favorites, while his queen gardened and tended doves. The grounds boasted a secluded lodge and a forest reserved for hunting deer and other game. In the fields hundreds of workers cleared irrigation channels, raised and mended terrace walls, and sowed corn and a host of exotic crops. These provided Huayna Capac with bountiful harvests and enough corn beer to entertain his subjects royally during Cusco's annual festivals.

Quispiguanca was not the only spectacular estate. Inca kings inherited little more than their titles, so each new sovereign built a city palace and country home for himself and his lineage shortly after assuming power. To date archaeologists and historians have located ruins of roughly a dozen royal estates built by at least six Inca kings.

Even after these kings died, they remained the powers behind the throne. "The ancestors were a key element of Andean life," says Sonia Guillén, director of Peru's Museo Leymebamba. When Huayna Capac perished of a mysterious disease in Ecuador around 1527, retainers mummified his body and carried it back to Cusco. Members of the royal family frequently visited the deceased monarch, asking his advice on vital matters and heeding the replies given by an oracle sitting at his side. Years after his death, Huayna Capac remained the owner of Quispiguanca and the surrounding estate. Indeed, royal tradition dictated that its harvest keep his mummy, servants, wives, and descendants in style for eternity.

It was during the rainy season in 1533, an auspicious time for a coronation, and thousands of people were packed into the main plaza of Cusco to celebrate the arrival of their new teenage king. Two years earlier, amid a civil war, foreign invaders had landed in the north. Metal-clad and bearing lethal new weapons, the Spaniards had (Continued on page 94)

The terraced pools of mineral-laden water at Maras produce salt by evaporation, as they did in the time of the Inca. The ancient community nearby was called Kachi, "salt" in the local language.

(Continued from page 91) journeyed to the northern Inca town of Cajamarca, where they took prisoner the Inca king, Atahuallpa. Eight months later, they executed their royal captive, and in 1533 their leader, Francisco Pizarro, picked a young prince, Manco Inca Yupanqui, to rule as a puppet king.

In the far distance, voices of the young king's bearers echoed through the streets, singing songs of praise. Falling silent, celebrants watched the royal teenager enter the square, accompanied by the mummies of his ancestors, each richly attired and seated on a splendid litter. The wizened kings and their consorts reminded all that Manco Inca descended from a long line of kings. Rulers of other realms might content themselves with displaying carved or painted images of their glorious ancestors. The Inca kings went one better, displaying the expertly preserved bodies of their forefathers.

In the months that followed, the Spanish invaders seized the palaces of Cusco and the spacious country estates and took royal women as mistresses and wives. Incensed, Manco Inca rebelled and in 1536 tried to drive them from the realm. When his army suffered defeat, he fled Cusco for the jungle city of Vilcabamba, from which he launched guerrilla attacks. The Spanish wouldn't subdue the stronghold until 1572.

In the turmoil of those decades, the Inca's sprawling network of roads, storehouses, temples, and estates began slowly falling into ruin. As the empire crumbled, the Inca and their descendants made a valiant attempt to preserve the symbols of imperial authority. Servants collected the precious bodies of the sacred kings and concealed them around Cusco, where they were worshiped in secret—and in defiance of Spanish priests. In 1559 Cusco's chief magistrate, Juan Polo de Ondegardo, resolved to stamp out this idolatry. He launched an official search for

Can you imagine how American citizens would feel if the British had taken the bodies of the first several presidents back to London during the War of 1812?

the bodies, questioning hundreds. With this information he tracked down and seized the remains of 11 Inca kings and several queens.

For a time colonial officials in Lima displayed the mummies of Pachacutec, Huayna Capac, and two other royals as curiosities in the Hospital of San Andrés in Lima, a facility that admitted only European patients. But the damp coastal climate wreaked havoc with the bodies. So Spanish officials buried the greatest of the Inca kings in secrecy in Lima, far from the Andes and the people who loved and worshipped them.

In 2001 Brian Bauer and two Peruvian colleagues, historian Teodoro Hampe Martínez and archaeologist Antonio Coello Rodríguez, went looking for the mummies of the Inca kings, hoping to right a historic wrong and restore to Peruvians an important part of their cultural heritage. "Can you imagine," Bauer asks, "how American citizens would feel if the British had taken the bodies of the first several presidents back to London during the War of 1812?"

For months Bauer and his colleagues pored over old architectural plans of the Hospital of San Andrés, now a girls' school in central Lima. Eventually they identified several possibilities for the burial site of Pachacutec and Huayna Capac. Using ground-penetrating radar, they scanned the likeliest areas, turning up what appeared to be a vaulted underground crypt. Bauer and his Peruvian teammates were thrilled.

When the archaeologists finally dug down and opened the door of the dusty chamber, they were crestfallen. The crypt lay empty. Quite possibly, says Bauer, workmen removed the contents while renovating the hospital after a severe earthquake. Today no one can say where Peru's greatest kings lie. Concludes Bauer sadly, "The fate of the royal Inca mummies remains unknown."

Discussion Questions:

- How did Dr. Bauer's survey work in the Valley of Cusco change archaeologists' understanding of when the Inca Empire first began to rise?

- What were the social and political factors that led to the Inca's ability to dominate wide portions of South America?

- What was the importance of mummified remains, especially those of past leaders, to the Inca people? How did Europeans attempt to reduce this importance?

Archaeological Interpretations:

- How are archaeologists reconstructing the deep history of the Incas? What sort of data are they using and how are they finding it?

- What is the importance of determining the precise timing and history surrounding the rise of the Incas? How does this determination affect our understanding of the causal affects of power centralization?

Paradigm Creation:
Material Basis of Power and Organizational Needs of Empire

- What were the material factors that underwrote the beginnings of power consolidation in the Cusco Valley?

- In your own words, describe how the Inca empire was based on economic, political, and organizational practices and how these different aspects of society worked together to mobilize and centralize power.

- What was the place of cosmological beliefs for the Inca elite, particularly the importance of ancestry?

DIVINING ANGKOR

Divining Angkor is largely about how cities/urban centers rise and fall based on human action and environmental affordances. Recent archaeological research suggests that irrigation practices, along with favorable weather conditions, provided the basis for the rise of Angkor as a highly populated and powerful cultural center during the 9th to 15th centuries C.E. The dramatic collapse in population and prestige that occurred at the end of Angkor appears to be related to a complicated amalgam of shifting weather patterns, changing religious beliefs, and hostile neighbors. Archaeologists continue to unravel the history of this site through directed excavations and analysis of materials.

When reading this article, you should focus on:

- How do environmental conditions and cultural innovations work together to provide opportunities for the establishment of urban centers?
- How are urban centers more or less susceptible to changing social and natural factors?
- What role did religious beliefs have in the history of Angkor Wat?
- How do archaeologists reconstruct past weather patterns?
- Why are cultural responses to environmental shifts important to the long-term survival of the society?

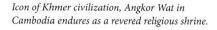

Icon of Khmer civilization, Angkor Wat in Cambodia endures as a revered religious shrine.

DIVINING
ANGKOR

By Richard Stone
Photographs by Robert Clark

For local boys the moat at Angkor Wat is a swimming hole. In the 12th century it symbolized the oceans encircling the home of the gods. It also had a practical use: storing water for the city's large population.

Once viewed solely as a sacred site with a temple in its middle, the five-mile-long West Baray is also understood as a hub of a vast water-management system, crucial to Angkor's wealth

AFTER RISING TO SUBLIME HEIGHTS,
THE SACRED CITY
MAY HAVE ENGINEERED ITS OWN DOWNFALL.

From the air, the centuries-old temple appears and vanishes like a hallucination. At first it is no more than an umber smudge in the forest canopy of northern Cambodia. Beneath us sprawls the lost city of Angkor, now in ruins and populated mostly by peasant rice farmers. Clusters of Khmer homes, perched on spindly stilts to cope with flooding during the summer monsoon, dot the landscape from the Tonle Sap, the "great lake" of Southeast Asia, some 20 miles to the south, to the Kulen Hills, a ridge jutting from the floodplain a roughly equal distance to the north. Then, as Donald Cooney guides the ultralight plane over the treetops, the magnificent temple comes into view.

Restored in the 1940s, the 12th-century Banteay Samre, devoted to the Hindu god Vishnu, recalls the medieval Khmer Empire at its height. The temple is cloistered inside two sets of concentric square walls. These may once have been surrounded by a moat symbolizing the oceans encircling Mount Meru, mythical home of Hindu gods. Banteay Samre is just one of more than a thousand shrines the Khmer erected in the city of Angkor during a

Angkor is the scene of one of the greatest vanishing acts of all time.

building spree whose scale and ambition rivals the pyramids of Egypt. After we pass, I crane my neck for a last look. The temple has disappeared into the forest.

Angkor is the scene of one of the greatest vanishing acts of all time. The Khmer kingdom lasted from the ninth to the 15th centuries, and at its height dominated a wide swath of Southeast Asia, from Myanmar (Burma) in the west to Vietnam in the east. As many as 750,000 people lived in Angkor, its capital, which sprawled across an area the size of New York City's five boroughs, making it the most extensive urban complex of the preindustrial world. By the late 16th century, when Portuguese missionaries came upon the lotus-shaped towers of Angkor Wat—the most elaborate of the city's temples and the world's largest religious monument—the once resplendent capital of the empire was in its death throes.

Scholars have come up with a long list of suspected causes, including rapacious invaders, a religious change of heart, and a shift to

Adapted from "Diving Angkor" by Richard Stone: National Geographic Magazine, July 2009.

Lotus flowers and Hindu deities carved in stone mark the holy site of Kbal Spean in the Kulen Hills, the source of two rivers that nourish the Angkor floodplain.

maritime trade that condemned an inland city. It's mostly guesswork: Roughly 1,300 inscriptions survive on temple doorjambs and freestanding stelae, but the people of Angkor left not a single word explaining their kingdom's collapse.

Recent excavations, not of the temples but of the infrastructure that made the vast city possible, are converging on a new answer. Angkor, it appears, was doomed by the very ingenuity that transformed a collection of minor fiefdoms into an empire. The civilization learned how to tame Southeast Asia's seasonal deluges, then faded as its control of water, the most vital of resources, slipped away.

An intriguing firsthand account brings the city to life at its zenith. Zhou Daguan, a Chinese diplomat, spent nearly a year in the capital at the end of the 13th century. He lived modestly as a guest of a middle-class family who ate rice using coconut-husk spoons and drank wine made from honey, leaves, or rice. He described a gruesome practice, abandoned not long before his visit, that involved collecting human gall from living donors as a tonic for courage. Religious festivals featured fireworks and boar fighting. The greatest spectacles occurred when the king ventured out among his subjects. Royal processions included elephants and horses decorated with gold, and hundreds of palace women bedecked in flowers.

Angkor's daily rhythms also come to life in sculptures that have survived centuries of decay and, more recently, war. Bas-reliefs on temple facades depict everyday scenes—two men hunched over a board game, for instance, and a woman giving birth under a shaded pavilion—and pay homage to the spiritual world inhabited by creatures such as *apsaras,* alluring celestial dancers who served as messengers between humans and the gods.

The bas-reliefs also reveal trouble in paradise. Interspersed with visions of earthly harmony and sublime enlightenment are scenes of war. In one bas-relief, spear-bearing warriors from the neighboring kingdom of Champa are packed stem to stern in a boat crossing the Tonle Sap. The scene is immortalized in stone, of course, because the Khmer were successful in battle.

Although Angkor won that clash, the city was riven by rivalry, which heightened its vulnerability to attacks from Champa to the east and the formidable kingdom of Ayutthaya to the west. Khmer kings had several wives, which blurred the line of succession and resulted in constant intrigue as princes vied for power. "For centuries, it was like the Wars of the Roses. The Khmer state was often unstable," says Roland Fletcher, an archaeologist at the University of Sydney and co-director of a research effort called the Greater Angkor Project.

Some scholars believe that Angkor died the way it lived: by the sword. The annals of Ayutthaya state that warriors from that kingdom "took" Angkor in 1431. No doubt the prosperous Khmer city would have been a rich prize: Inscriptions boast that its temple towers were clad in gold, as Zhou's breathless account confirms. To reconcile tales of Angkor's wealth with the dilapidated ruins encountered by Western travelers, French historians a century ago concluded from the tantalizing allusion that Ayutthaya sacked Angkor.

Fletcher, who says his obsession is to "figure out what makes settlements grow and die," is dubious. Some early scholars, he says, viewed Angkor through the lens of the sieges and conquests of European history. "The ruler of Ayutthaya, indeed, says he took Angkor, and he may have taken some formal regalia back to Ayutthaya with him," says Fletcher. But after Angkor was captured, Ayutthaya's ruler installed his son on the throne. "He's not likely to have smashed the place up before giving it to his son."

Royal processions included elephants and horses decorated with gold, and hundreds of palace women bedecked in flowers.

Court intrigue may not have perturbed most of Angkor's subjects, but religion was central to daily life. Angkor was what anthropologists call a regal-ritual city. Its kings claimed to be the world emperors of Hindu lore and erected temples to themselves. But as Theravada Buddhism gradually eclipsed Hinduism in the 13th and 14th centuries, its tenet of social equality may have threatened Angkor's elite. "It was very subversive, just like Christianity was subversive to the Roman Empire," says Fletcher. "It would have been exceedingly difficult to stop."

Such a religious shift would have eroded royal authority. The regal-ritual city operated on a moneyless economy, relying on tribute and taxation. The kingdom's de facto currency was rice, staple of the conscripted laborers who built the temples and the cast of thousands who ran them. An inscription at one complex, Ta Prohm, notes that 12,640 people serviced that temple alone. The inscription also records that more than 66,000 farmers produced nearly 3,000 tons of rice a year to feed this multitude of priests, dancers, and temple workers. Add just three large temples to the equation—Preah Khan and the larger complexes of Angkor Wat and the Bayon—and the calculated farm labor required swells to 300,000. That's nearly half of the estimated population of Greater Angkor. A new, egalitarian religion such as Theravada Buddhism might have led to rebellion.

Or maybe the royal court simply turned its back on Angkor. Successive rulers had a habit of erecting new temple complexes and letting older ones decay, and that penchant for starting anew might have doomed the city when sea trade began to flourish between Southeast Asia and China. Maybe it was simple economic opportunism that, by the 16th century, had caused the Khmer center of power to shift to a location closer to the Mekong River, near Cambodia's present-day capital, Phnom

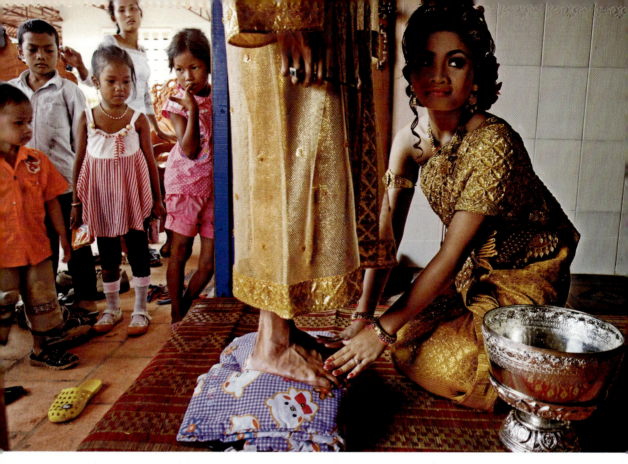

Resembling the apsaras, the beautiful dancers who appear on many of Angkor's temple walls, 17-year-old Sonsa Ry bends to tradition and washes her husband's feet at their wedding in the village of Thnal Toteung.

Penh, affording it easier access to the South China Sea.

Economic and religious turmoil may have hastened Angkor's downfall, but its rulers were blindsided by another foe. Angkor became a medieval powerhouse thanks to a sophisticated system of canals and reservoirs that enabled the city to hoard scarce water in dry months and disperse excess water during the rainy season. Forces beyond Angkor's control threw this exquisitely tuned machine into disarray.

One of Angkor's holiest sites is high in the Kulen Hills at the headwaters of two rivers, the Puok and the Siem Reap. Under the shade of gnarled strangler fig trees, submerged in the clear water of a lazy creek, are row after row of circular bumps, each about six inches wide, carved into the dark sandstone riverbed. These are worn lingams, cylindrical stone sculptures representing the essence of the Hindu god Shiva. The lingams lead like a road to another sculpture in the riverbed: a thick-walled square, a yard wide, with a narrow inlet. It's a yoni, a symbol of the Hindu source of life.

Angkor's high priests came here to thank the gods for providing the lifeblood of the kingdom. A short walk upstream is a natural bridge of sandstone that lends this holy site its name, Kbal Spean—Khmer for "bridgehead." Water rushes through a cleft, splashing an adjoining rock face where Vishnu, legs crossed, meditates atop an angry ocean; sprouting from his navel is a lotus-flower-bearing Brahma. Here in the Kulen Hills the ancient gods enjoy perpetual libations from flowing water.

By harnessing the monsoon tide that gushed from the Kulen Hills, Angkor and its rulers flourished. From the era of Jayavarman II, who laid the kingdom's foundations in the early 800s, the empire's growth depended on bumper rice harvests. Throughout southern Asia, perhaps only the ancient cities of Anuradhapura and Polonnaruwa in Sri Lanka and their famed reservoirs could compare to Angkor's ability to guarantee a steady water supply.

That reliability required massive feats of engineering, including a reservoir called the West Baray that's five miles long and 1.5 miles wide. To build this third and most sophisticated of Angkor's large reservoirs a thousand years ago, as many as 200,000 Khmer workers may have been needed to pile up nearly 16 million cubic yards of soil in embankments 300 feet wide and three stories tall. To this day the rectangular reservoir, or *baray,* is fed by water diverted from the Siem Reap River.

The first scholar to appreciate the scale of Angkor's waterworks was Bernard-Philippe Groslier, an archaeologist with the French School of Asian Studies (EFEO). In a landmark 1979 treatise, he envisioned Angkor as a "hydraulic city." The great barays, he argued, served two purposes: to symbolize the primeval sea of Hindu cosmogony and to irrigate rice fields. Unfortunately, Groslier could not pursue this concept further. Cambodia's civil war, the brutal reign of the Khmer Rouge, and the ouster of the regime by Vietnamese forces in 1979 turned Angkor into a no-go zone for two decades. After Vietnamese troops withdrew, looters descended on Angkor, swiping statues and even chiseling off bas-reliefs.

When Christophe Pottier, an architect and archaeologist, reopened EFEO's research station at Angkor in 1992, the first priority was helping Cambodia restore dilapidated and pillaged temples. But Pottier was drawn to the wilderness beyond the temple walls. He spent

We realized that the entire landscape of Greater Angkor is artificial. It was an **incredibly clever** system.

months crisscrossing the southern half of Greater Angkor on motorbike and foot, mapping once hidden house mounds and shrines near artificial ponds called water tanks. (Lingering lawlessness deterred Pottier from surveying the northern half.) Then, in 2000, Fletcher and his colleague Damian Evans laid hands on NASA radar images of Angkor. They were a revelation: The University of Sydney team, working with EFEO and APSARA, the Cambodian agency that manages Angkor, found vestiges of many more settlements, canals, and water tanks, particularly in Angkor's inaccessible areas. Donald Cooney's ultralight flights have helped Fletcher and Pottier, now a co-director of the Greater Angkor Project, examine these features in finer detail. Crucially, they found inlets and outlets to the barays, ending a debate catalyzed by Groslier's work about whether the colossal reservoirs were used solely for religious rituals or for irrigation. The clear answer is both.

The researchers were amazed by the ambition of Angkor's engineers. "We realized that the entire landscape of Greater Angkor is artificial," Fletcher says. Over several centuries, teams of laborers constructed hundreds of miles of canals and dikes that relied on subtle differences in the land's natural inclination to divert water from the Puok, Roluos, and Siem Reap Rivers to the barays. During the summer monsoon months, overflow channels bled off excess water. After the rains petered out in October or November, irrigation channels dispensed stored water. The barays may also have helped replenish soil moisture by allowing water to soak into the earth. In surrounding fields surface evaporation would have drawn up the groundwater to supply crops. "It was an incredibly clever system," says Fletcher.

That clever water system may have made the difference between mediocrity and greatness. Much of the kingdom's rice was grown in embanked fields that *(Continued on page 117)*

IMPERIAL ANGKOR

ITS VAST WATER SYSTEM WAS A MARVEL OF ENGINEERING—AND A CAUTIONARY TALE OF TECHNOLOGICAL OVERREACH.

At its height in the 13th century (depicted in this reconstruction), the capital of the Khmer Empire was the most extensive urban complex in the world. Using imaging radar and other tools, researchers have learned that Greater Angkor covered almost 400 square miles, roughly the area of the five boroughs of New York City, with as many as 750,000 inhabitants. Most were rice farmers and laborers who worked the giant jigsaw of fields. In the city center, perhaps 40,000 people—elites and farmers alike—lived within the walls of Angkor Thom, a 3.5-square-mile enclosure with temples and a royal palace. Though the rainy season usually brought ample water, the ability to store water in great reservoirs called barays and control its flow gave Angkor an edge in times of drought or flood. But this engineered landscape required constant maintenance. When the water system faltered, so did Angkor's power.

Nokor Pheas

West

West Baray

Wat Chedei

Phnom Krom

A

ASIA
CHINA
—TAIWAN
•CAMBODIA
EQUATOR
AUSTRALIA

ANGKOR'S COMPLEX PLUMBING

In Southeast Asia, months of monsoon rains are followed by months of near drought. To ensure a steady water supply, stabilize rice production, and control flooding, Khmer engineers built a network of canals, moats, ponds, and reservoirs. Massive earthworks slowed the wet-season deluge flowing from the Kulen Hills, directing it into canals that fed the barays and temple moats. Spreading across the gently sloping land, the water drained finally into the Tonle Sap, the largest freshwater lake in Southeast Asia.

SACRED SOURCE
The Kulen Hills sheltered the headwaters of the Siem Reap River and were quarried for rock to build Angkor's temples. The hills were logged for timber and firewood and to clear land for farming; deforestation may have caused floods that choked some of Angkor's canals with sand and silt.

RICE FIELDS

N

Banteay Srei

SPILLWAY DAM

Puok

Baphuon   Phimeanakas   **Angkor Thom**   Neak Pean   East Mebon

Thnal Toteung (modern)

Preah Khan

North Baray

East Baray

Bayon

Ta Keo   Ta Prohm   *Srah Srang*   Pre Rup

Banteay Samre

Phnom Bakheng

Angkor Wat

Prasat Kravan

Roluo

Siem Reap (modern)

R I C E   F I E L D S

F L O O D E D   R I C E   F I E L D S

F L O O D E D   F O R E S T

ART BY STEVE COWDEN. INSET ART BY TOM CHANDLER AND MICHAEL LIM, MONASH UNIVERSITY
M. BRODY DITTEMORE AND LISA R. RITTER, NG STAFF. BASE MAP DATA BY DAMIAN EVANS, UNIVERSITY
OF SYDNEY, AND CHRISTOPHE POTTIER, FRENCH SCHOOL OF ASIAN STUDIES (EFEO)
CONSULTANT: ROLAND FLETCHER, UNIVERSITY OF SYDNEY

SOURCES: EFEO; GREATER ANGKOR PROJECT, A COLLABORATION OF APSARA, EFEO,
AND UNIVERSITY OF SYDNEY SCALE VARIES IN THIS PERSPECTIVE. LENGTH OF EAST BARAY IS 4.5 MI (7.2 KM).

Tonle Sap

Strangler-fig trees and creeping lichens devour ruins at Ta Prohm, once home to hundreds of monks. To build their magnificent complexes, Angkor's feudal rulers relied on revenue generated by rice growing.

Monsoon clouds spill rain into the Srah Srang reservoir. Its guardians included lions and flame-shaped nagas, spirits trusted to bring rain. By the 16th century power shifted from Angkor toward Phnom Penh after a period of erratic monsoons.

Only kings and high priests could worship atop the hill temple of Phnom Bakheng. Now reverent silence reigns only after closing time. Sunset-viewing tourists crowd onto the platform in numbers that cause structural damage.

Come November (top), villagers float instead of walk as the lake, home of one of the world's richest inland fisheries, brims at high water, and families easily net dinner from their porches.

For centuries the coming and going of water has shaped the lives of villagers near Tonle Sap. In early July (bottom), before the lake rises, houses built on 20-foot stilts stand high and dry in Kompong Phluk.

(Continued from page 105) would otherwise have relied on monsoon rains or the seasonal ebb and flow of water on the Tonle Sap floodplain. Irrigation would have boosted harvests. The system could also have provided survival rations during a poor monsoon season, says Fletcher. And the ability to divert and impound water would have afforded a measure of protection from floods. When other kingdoms in Southeast Asia were struggling to cope with too little or too much water, he says, Angkor's waterworks would have been "a profoundly valuable strategic asset."

Thus Fletcher was baffled when his team unearthed one of the more extraordinary pieces of Angkorian workmanship—a vast structure in the waterworks—and found that it had been demolished, apparently by Angkor's own engineers.

It's almost noon on a June day about ten miles north of Angkor Wat, and even at the bottom of a muddy, 14-foot-long trench, there's no relief from the fierce sun. Fletcher takes off a dark blue baseball cap and wipes his brow. It looks as if the self-possessed researcher is going to launch into a precise explanation of the grayish red stone blocks his team, along with Chhay Rachna of APSARA, has unearthed. Instead, he sighs and says, "This is simply fantastic!"

The stone blocks fitting snugly together were hewed from laterite, a spongy, iron-laden soil that hardens when exposed to air. When Fletcher and Pottier first found a section of the structure a few years ago, they thought it was the remains of a small sluice gate.

"It's turned into a monster," he says. The blocks are the remnants of a spillway across a sloping dam that may have extended as long as a football field. Around the end of the ninth century, with Angkor blossoming,

Bas-reliefs depict everyday scenes—men hunched over a board game, a woman giving birth. **They also reveal trouble in paradise.**

engineers excavated a long canal that altered the course of the Siem Reap River, redirecting it southward to the newly constructed East Baray, a reservoir nearly as big as the later West Baray. The dam, positioned in the river, diverted water to feed the canal. But part of the massive structure may also have functioned as a spillway during monsoon surges, when water would have overtopped the low structure and flowed down the former river channel.

The ruins of the spillway are a vital clue to an epic struggle that unfolded as generations of Khmer engineers coped with a water system that grew ever more complex and unruly. "They probably spent vast portions of their lives fixing it," says Fletcher. Some of the dam's blocks lie in a jumble; huge sections of masonry are missing. "The most logical explanation is that the dam failed," Fletcher says. The river may have chewed into the dam, gradually weakening it. Perhaps it was washed away by an unusually heavy flood, the kind that comes along every century or even every 500 years. The Khmer then ripped apart much of the remaining stonework, salvaging the blocks for other purposes.

Another clue that the water system was failing comes from a pond at the West Mebon, an island temple in the middle of the West Baray. Pollen grains preserved in the muck show that lotuses and other aquatic plants flourished in the baray until the early 13th century. Then new kinds of pollen appear, from species such as ferns that prefer marsh or dry land. Right at Angkor's zenith, one of its reservoirs apparently went dry for a time. "Something was going wrong much earlier than we expected," says Daniel Penny, a pollen expert and a co-director of the Greater Angkor Project.

Any deterioration of the waterworks would have left Angkor vulnerable to a natural

Gamblers gather for a cockfight. A crocodile hunts for fish. A war canoe advances. Carvings at the Bayon temple record events large and small from Angkor's past.

phenomenon no engineer of that day could have anticipated. Starting in the 1300s, Europe endured a few centuries of unpredictable weather marked by harsh winters and chilly summers. Until recently there was only sketchy information on how other parts of the world fared during this period, called the Little Ice Age. Now it appears that Southeast Asia, too, experienced climatic upheaval.

Around Angkor, the summer monsoon season lasts from roughly May through October and delivers nearly 90 percent of the region's yearly precipitation. A dependable monsoon is critical for all manner of life, including people. To unmask monsoon patterns of long ago, Brendan Buckley of the Lamont-Doherty Earth Observatory in Palisades, New York, ventured into the forests of Southeast Asia in search of trees with annual growth rings. He and his team knew it would not be easy: Most species in the region lack distinguishable growth rings or have ones that aren't laid down year by year. Several forays paid off with a clutch of long-lived species, including teak and *po mu,* a rare cypress. Some po mu trees they cataloged are nine centuries old, survivors of both Angkor's heyday and its demise.

The po mu trees told a stunning story. Sets of constricted growth rings showed that the trees had endured back-to-back megadroughts, from 1362 to 1392 and from 1415 to 1440. During these periods the monsoon was weak or delayed, and in some years it may have failed completely. In other years, megamonsoons lashed the region.

To a tottering kingdom, extreme weather could have been the coup de grâce. Decades earlier, Angkor's waterworks were already ailing, to judge from the idled West Baray. "We don't know why the water system was operating below capacity—it's a conundrum," says Penny. "But what it means is that Angkor really had no fat to burn. The city was more exposed to the threat of drought than at any other time in its history." Prolonged and severe droughts, punctuated by torrential downpours, "would have ruined the water system," says Fletcher.

Still, Penny says, "we're not talking about the place becoming a desert." People on the Tonle Sap floodplain south of the main temples would have been buffered from the worst effects. The Tonle Sap is fed by the Mekong River, whose headwaters in Tibetan glacier fields would have been largely immune to the effects of an altered monsoon. But Khmer engineers, skilled as they were, could not alleviate parched conditions in the north by moving Tonle Sap water against the lay of the land. Gravity was their only pump.

If inhabitants of northern Angkor were starving while other parts of the city were hoarding rice, the stage would have been set for severe unrest. "When populations in tropical countries exceed the carrying capacity of the land, real trouble begins," says Yale University anthropologist Michael Coe. "This inevitably leads to cultural collapse." A malnourished army, preoccupied with internal strife, would have exposed the city to attack. Indeed, Ayutthaya's invasion and the Khmer king's ouster happened near the end of the second megadrought.

Add to the climate chaos the shifting political and religious winds already buffeting

Angkor, it appears, was **doomed by the very ingenuity** that transformed a collection of minor fiefdoms into an empire.

the kingdom, and Angkor's fate was sealed, says Fletcher. "The world around Angkor was changing. Society was moving on. It would have been a surprise if Angkor persisted."

The Khmer Empire was not the first civilization felled by climate catastrophe. Centuries earlier, as Angkor was rising, halfway around the world a similar loss of environmental equilibrium was hammering the Maya city-states in Mexico and Central America. Many scholars now believe that the Maya succumbed to overpopulation and environmental degradation following a series of three punishing droughts in the ninth century. "Essentially, the same thing happened to Angkor," says Coe, who in the 1950s was the first to discern similarities between the Khmer and Maya civilizations.

Modern societies may need to brace for similar climatic challenges. According to Buckley, the most likely trigger of the Angkor megadroughts was intense and persistent El Niño warming of the surface waters of the central and eastern tropical Pacific Ocean. Scientists debate whether human-caused climate change will lead to more pronounced El Niños, but the Vietnamese tree rings show that even natural oscillations in the Pacific can spark catastrophe.

Angkor's end is a sobering lesson in the limits of human ingenuity. The Khmer had transformed their world—a monumental investment that would have been excruciating for the kingdom's rulers to forsake. "Angkor's hydraulic system was an amazing machine, a wonderful mechanism for regulating the world," Fletcher says. Its engineers managed to keep the civilization's signal achievement running for six centuries—until, in the end, a greater force overwhelmed them.

Dynasties rise and fall, but fish and rice are constants in Khmer daily life. As floodwaters ebb from a paddy field near Angkor Wat, Lao Lan sizes up his catch at a fish barrier. Not enough to sell, he says, but enough to eat.

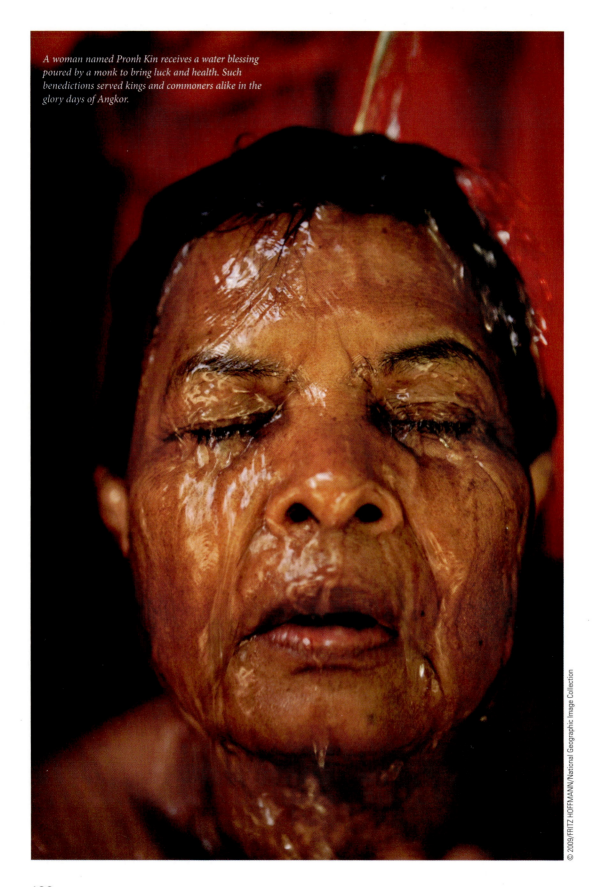

A woman named Pronh Kin receives a water blessing poured by a monk to bring luck and health. Such benedictions served kings and commoners alike in the glory days of Angkor.

Discussion Questions:

- According to the article, what were the environmental factors that contributed to the rise of Angkor Wat? What were the cultural/social factors?

- How do the recent archaeological investigations within the waterways of Angkor provide evidence of why this city was eventually abandoned?

- What might residents and leaders of modern cities learn from the demise of Angkor? In particular, how might cities facing changing natural conditions, such as global warming, benefit from a better understanding of this ancient city?

- In what ways are urban centers, such an Angkor, especially susceptible to collapse?

Archaeological Interpretations:

- What types of data were used by archaeologists to reconstruct past environmental and social conditions? How were these data-sets collected?

- How did archaeologists analyze and interpret these data-sets in order to better understand the weather conditions, political decision-making, and cultural innovations taking place during the history of Angor Wat?

- How applicable are the interpretations drawn from Angor Wat to cities/urban centers in general? Do you think that the conclusions regarding the rise and fall of this early city are unique to Angor Wat, or are there broader lessons that can be applied to help better understand other ancient cities? What about applying these lessons to modern cities?

Paradigm Creation:
Cultural Decision-Making and Environmental Conditions

- The article suggests many factors that possibly contributed to both the rise and fall of Angor Wat–what were these factors? Which of these factors might be considered cultural? Which are natural?

- In your own words, describe how the article suggests natural and cultural factors worked together to bring Angor Wat to a position of power, as well as how it eventually collapsed.

- Do you think that changing environmental conditions made it impossible for Angor Wat to continue as a powerful urban center, or was it feasible to avert disaster with better decision making? Do you feel that the article gave too much/ too little/ just the right amount of emphasis on the natural conditions surrounding the rise and fall of Angor? What other information might you like to have in order to better understand the history of Angor?